I0568435

SCARS
UNVEILED

SYDELLE RICARDO

Coach: Drs Luisette Kraal.

www.Luisettekraal.com

ISBN: 978-1-960509-26-0

Sydelle Ricardo

CONTENTS

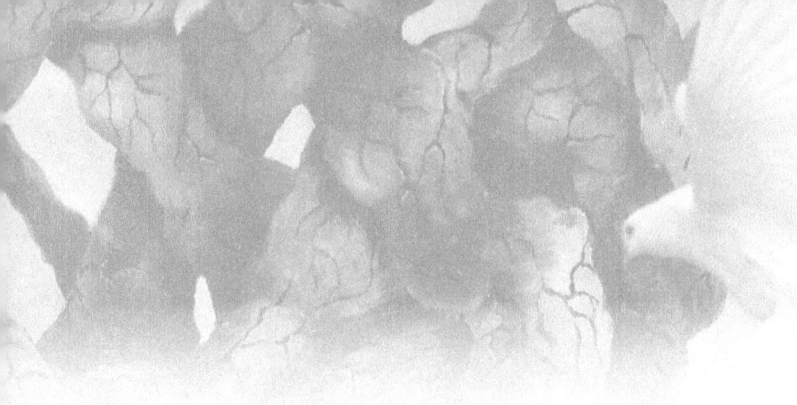

INSPIRED BY SHANA'S STORY

"It burns through my skin like oil on fire It penetrates the depths of my soul and it intertwines with my spirit. It affects who I truly am and pushes me toward who I will become. It paralyzes me with fear and shame. I lost my innocence... way too soon."

~ Sydelle Ricardo ~

1. INNOCENCE

When I was a little girl, my mom and dad were everything to me. They gave me a sense of security. When I think of my parents, my heart fills with emotion. I can almost feel my hand brushing against my mom's soft, caramel-colored skin. My mother, tall and graceful, stood beside my father, who was handsome and kind. In the eyes of many, they were a proud, stylish couple.

My mother flew to Miami from the Caribbean island of Curaçao at least four times a year to buy beautiful, high-quality, fashionable clothes to sell and of course, for us to wear. I can't remember a single moment when she wasn't doing that! She took me everywhere. I was like an extension of her. Wherever she went, I followed. Whether to the pharmacy or to the bookstore Mensing's Caminada, I was right there beside her. Even if we went to the store for just one thing, we always left with more. I would watch her closely, observing her with wide eyes until tears filled mine. But my mom was also strict and would discipline us when necessary.

My father, on the other hand, never really got angry with us. As far back as I can remember, he punished me only once and then he quickly came back to check on me, bringing me sweets to comfort me in my room. He was the one who drove us around in his stylish car, always well-dressed and strong. He liked to attract attention. He was my hero, and I loved joking around with him!

Both my parents had great taste for everything beautiful and elegant.

They loved European perfumes that smelled divine. Life was good. Whatever I needed, I received: clothes, shoes, toys and especially my favorite... Barbie dolls.

I loved playing with dolls. For birthdays, Easter, or any special occasion, if someone asked me what I wanted, my answer was always the same: a Barbie or something for my Barbies. I had a kitchen set, a car, a horse, Ken, a bed... all from the official 'Mattel' brand. I created a whole Barbie world under my desk. Everything I saw in real life, I recreated for my Barbies with my imagination. I built an ideal world for them.

The outside world? I brought it into my room and blended it with my fantasy into a world that didn't exist. A world inside my head. A world where everything was perfect! A fantasy where nothing bad ever happened. In my fantasy world, there was always a happy ending. No evil existed. I saw everything through rose-colored glasses. Pink, because it was my favorite color, and all my Barbie things were pink too. Everything had to include pink. My room was pink and white. To me, pink meant: "little girl" just beautiful.

In my room, where I spent so much time, I could live for hours in my fantasy world. My best friend, who lived next door, loved playing Barbie with me. He especially liked playing with Ken, Barbie's husband. We never got bored. The role-playing fascinated us, and time flew.

Until my Nana's loud voice echoed through the house, telling my friend to go home. Game over! When Nana spoke, the whole house heard it! Her voice sounded like the carnival-season drums and church bells ringing at the same time. Nana would ask my friend, "Don't you have a home?"

Our house had four bedrooms, each with its own bathroom. All the bedrooms were on the right side of the house. Up front was my parents' master bedroom. Then came my stepsister Judy's room and bathroom, followed by mine, and then my brother Bryan's room and bath. My room and Bryan's had separate entrances. One led to the back balcony, the other outside into the yard. A corridor connected all the rooms.

When we were in our rooms with the lights off, the light from the hallway would shine from under our doors. That light meant so much to me. I didn't like sleeping in the dark. But that little strip of hallway light that was glowing under my door brought me peace. A light I could focus on. It eased me. That light made my room feel less dark. It gave me a sense of safety. Later, I would realize how symbolic that light was in the years to come.

As I got older, our home in the neighborhood, Mahaai, became something of a hangout for young people. Groups of kids would stop by after school, sometimes still in uniform or barefoot. Playing hide and seek, goofing off on the balcony with fresh juice and snacks. We'd toast bread with butter and cheese - better than any toaster snack nowadays - and indulged ourselves with fruit.

All that fruit came straight from the trees in our yard. There were trees with surinam cherries, soursop, sapodilla, mango, banana, lime, and tamarind. The tamarind tree belonged to our neighbor, but its branches hung in our yard, so it felt like ours too. But one tree that stayed in my memory, deep in my soul, was the flamboyant tree. It feels just like yesterday that my friend and I were hanging from its branches like we were training for the Olympics.

Its branches were big and strong enough for both of us to hang on without breaking the branches. We'd sit in it, chit chatting, feeling safe among the birds and bugs. And when we were done, we'd leap off with flair. We'd land in a soft squatting pose before collapsing flat, limbs stretched out. Arms high in the air, like Nadia Comăneci: the famous Romanian gymnast from the 1976 Olympics, just after finishing her routine. We would run around the yard until we heard that familiar voice calling out - again - to ask if my friend didn't have a home to go to.

That tree stood in the middle of our yard. In my memory, it was massive. When it bloomed, it had a strong but sweet smell. The petals were green on the outside, but when they opened, they revealed a bright, coral-red flower. It had soft, powdery pollen that would stain your clothes. The branches were rough but gentle. Hard yet smooth under my little feet. We spent hours there. My parents even had a big round concrete porch built beneath it. That's where we stayed, hidden in its shade.

Years later, when I returned as an adult to see the house, I realized the yard that once felt like an endless field was actually relatively small. With my cousins, siblings, and my brother's neighborhood friends, who soon became mine, we shared so many joyful moments there. Every weekend, every school break, the house was full of young people. At the beginning of our teenage years, we socialized and shared life in our own special way. Life was good. Life was sweet... we were living in the fullness of our youth and innocence.

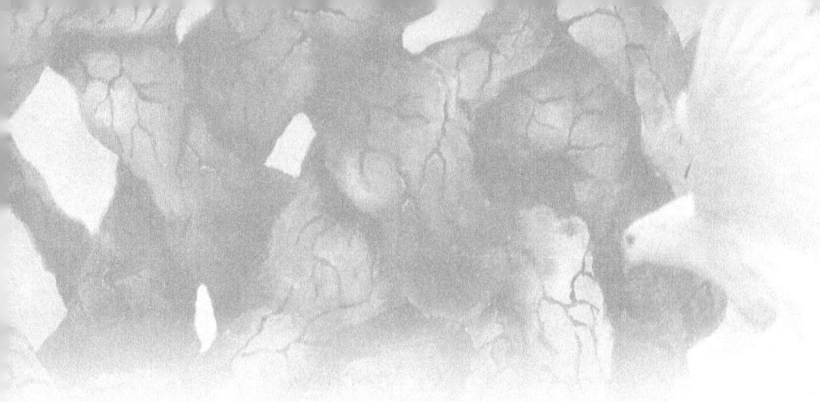

IT CAN'T BE TRUE!

Even though it is reality
Still, my mind refuses to process it.
Yes, I know it's a fact
But still, my heart refuses to accept it.
I reject my own reality
To try to hold on to what I've lost...
Just a little longer.
Maybe if I do that, I can control my pain?
Pretending everything stayed the same?
My inner battle is so intense
Sometimes faking it wins...
But reality is relentless
And always finds a way to break through.
My desperation grows,
It gets heavier each day,

And fear keeps haunting me like a shadow.
I'm a prisoner in my own situation
And I don't have the key to this prison.
Please! Help me find the key.
Because... even if it doesn't look like it
Deep down in my heart
There lives a longing...
That one day... I'll be free.
Please, help me find the key.

2. BURN MARKS

At noon, we would watch all kinds of soap stories: "Topacio", "Maite", and "¿What happened to Jaqueline?" Lies, tragedies, manipulation, family drama, rooted in love between two people who wanted to be together but were kept apart by something or someone.

These soap stories weren't just a novelty on the island, they were a whole world of their own. And their theme songs, sung by Latin American artists like Ricardo Montaner and José Luis Rodríguez, echoed in our homes and our hearts. Even today, those melodies take us right back. They sang with a kind of passion and emotion that could lift your soul and break it at the same time.

Everything new drew us in. We were curious about what we didn't know. Things we had never seen or experienced. People who had never left the island suddenly had a window into other cultures and ways of life. Things they had only read about in books or magazines or imagined in their minds. Soap stories from TeleCuraçao - the national TV station, Venevisión and RCTV of Venezuela filled living rooms and bedrooms, pulling in cousins, siblings, neighbors. Just anyone close enough to hear.

When one episode ended, you could barely wait for the next. You found yourself glued to the screen, unable to move, just waiting to see what would happen in the next episode. No binge watching back then.

These stories were the opposite of the ones my neighbor-friend and I used to make up in my bedroom, where everything always ended in happiness and hope.

Then one day, for reasons that were never quite explained, we were told that one of our cousins would come live with us. He wasn't much older than me, in high school, while I was still in primary school. I was very close to my cousins. We didn't have a big age gap, and our parents always made sure we did a lot together.

At one point, we all used to go to my grandmother's house after school to spend the afternoons. They'd sleep over too. During that time, my parents had a house large enough to host us all, and so it was normal for the family to stay over.

My parents believed deeply in helping others, and that's what they taught us too. Always have something extra at home so you can share it. If you're not using something anymore, don't sell it but give it away. If someone needed a place to sleep, you gave them a bed and food. If someone didn't have a family, we became their family. I never once heard my parents say we were doing it for God's blessings or in hopes of something in return. No. We did it because it was the right thing to do. And many years later, I followed their example and realized consciously that it truly is better to give than to receive.

However, many times I have to force myself to bring my memories back. There are times when I try to remember my past, but I can't. Sadly, more often than not, all I feel is disappointment, because I can't remember the sweet things either. My mom had to remind me about our trip to Venezuela to buy my dress and accessories for my sweet sixteen party. My dad had to tell me how we went to a baseball game in Orlando. I need pictures to recall the past, because the memories don't come back on their own. I depend on others to remind me of the beautiful things I experienced because I can't bring them to mind. It's like they never happened.

Bryan, my neighbor Chelo, my cousins, and I would all sit together watching Soap stories. It was the first time I saw people kissing each other so intimately. Watching those scenes - short as they were - my heart would start racing. I felt both uncomfortable and curious when the characters' eyes met. I could feel the sensation rising through me. The hairs on my arms would stand up.

My cousin was more developed than I was, and like any young person, he had his own way of expressing his emerging sexuality. I don't know what exactly led to it - whether it was a glance, a question, or something he said - but somehow I ended up in a situation I didn't fully understand. We were watching a Soap episode, and at the end of it, I would find myself lying in the dark, on the floor, with him on top of me. What happened in between is a blur.

I've searched for clarity, but there are no answers. I feel helpless, because I don't remember enough. And so, many pieces of my childhood scattered. Lost in deep darkness.

Judy, my older sister, had moved out, and her room became the setting for our own Soap episode: one that ended in tragedy. My cousin would ask me to come to the room. He would kiss me and touch my body. I always lay on the floor, and he was on top. His weight pressed down on me, and it felt suffocating. Sometimes I felt like I was floating above myself, watching us from the ceiling. I would see myself lying there beneath him. I didn't know if it was real or a nightmare. A deep sadness would pull me back into my body. Each time, I would turn my head toward the door, closed tight. Under that door, the sliver of light would sneak in.

My cousin would ask me to perform oral sex on him. I would do it. I didn't like it at all. He would kiss and touch me, and I accepted it, though I didn't find pleasure in it. Afterward, we would leave the room and continue as if nothing happened. Again. And again. It became a pattern. A recurring nightmare of fear, heartbeats, and anxiety. Each time, I would stare again at that little strip of light beneath the door, my only comfort, even though it was a lie.

No one knew. No one could help me. My brother saw us once, but he pretended he didn't. And I never dared to open up, not to him, not to anyone.

Later... I would bathe. Again and again. Scrubbing my body until I couldn't anymore. Trying to wash off my shame. It felt disgusting, like I was wearing a used cloth I couldn't get clean. So I kept scrubbing till the point that my skin started burning, like raw open skin. On fire and exposed. It felt as if someone set me on fire and left me burning. Destroyed. Not worth looking at. I felt used. Abused. And surely, I no longer felt beautiful.

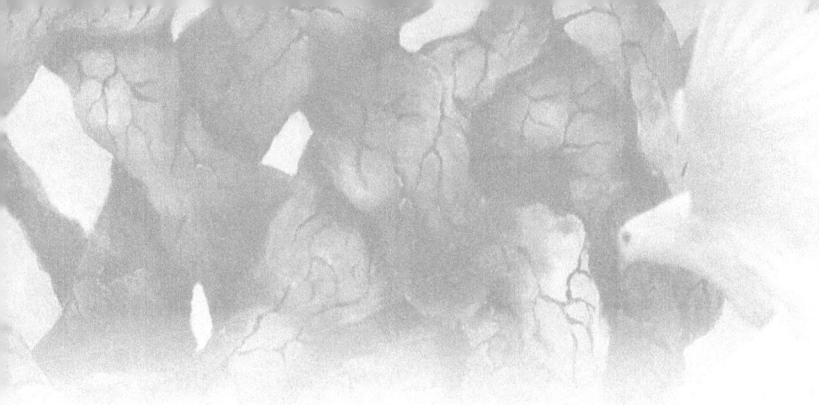

MY STRATEGY

What I knew all too well had taken place
In every way I tried to resist
Until I came to realize
That my effort would never be rewarded
It was in that dark moment of the soul
That anger was born
And I was sure that if I expressed it
My hunger for justice would be satisfied

But what I experienced was betrayal:
once again
I was sold out on the battlefield
And it seemed I didn't stand a chance
I tried to negotiate, hoping my
loss could be avoided

And when my pain became undeniable
So many plans started forming in my mind
If even just one word could win
Victory might help me forget
the pain of my loss?
But in vain... the battle continued
With my last bit of strength, I kept fighting
With my final breath, I screamed in
desperation
Is there someone who can
teach me the strategy
How to fight and win
Before I lose the last of my energy?
Please... teach me the strategy!

3. WATER FIRST

I used to spend a lot of time in the shower. I would stay under the water for long stretches, letting it run over my body. What I really wanted was for my skin to peel off. I didn't want to feel this rawness anymore. I wanted new skin. Clean. Untouched. I wanted the skin of my childhood and innocence back, that's what I wanted. But my skin didn't change, and I wasn't innocent anymore. I was part of soap serie filled with betrayal, bitterness, and grief. And like those on television, mine dragged on for years, even though the abuse had long stopped. The actions had ended, but they left behind wounds and scars no one could ever erase. My soul was marked forever.

My parents didn't understand why a girl who had always slept in her own room and on her own bed, now kept asking to sleep in theirs. Every night I got up and asked to lie down beside them. Between them. I was a teenager. Why would I want to sleep next to my parents? I had never needed that before. I was at an age where I was going out, and had my first boyfriend. I was in high school, talking and acting like every other teen. But I couldn't sleep alone anymore. The hallway light that once brought peace and comfort through the gap under the door, now exposed my truth. It shined on wounds I didn't want to see, much less show. Wounds left open, bleeding and biting, aching every hour of every day. The shame of being seen, the fear of being truly seen, took over my thoughts.

Fear that people might see me. Me! The daughter of respected parents with status and admiration. Me, who did so well in school, loving, warm, social, and practically everyone's friend. Me, who walked around with a bright smile and a heart to help others. Me, Shana! The sweet little beautiful dark-skinned girl, as they called me. The one with Indian features and curious eyes. Me, who loved God with everything in me. But the law of randomness had chosen me. And it whispered: "Why others, and not you?"

How could I speak the truth? How could I show what I had become, how to tell what had happened to me not once, but many times? Better not to say anything at all. No one would believe me anyway. They'd say I brought it on myself or claim it was nothing serious. They'd minimize what had happened, and I'd feel worse. Better to stay silent. I was going through something I didn't understand or know how to handle. It felt wrong, disgusting, pleasant, and confusing all at the same time. Pleasant because my body was responding. Physically, it sometimes felt okay, even familiar or comforting. And that only made it more complicated and worse.

How could something so wrong make my body feel pleasure? How could something meant to be shared in love with a partner become something dirty, traumatic, and twisted? Wicked! How could this happen with a cousin? someone meant to protect me? How could a family member become an abuser? What kind of horror is that? What madness? What devastation! I didn't know if I was crazy, or if this was simply how life worked. Where in my mind was I supposed to put this?

But still, I had to get up each day and keep living, like nothing had happened.

My mother, in her wisdom, noticed something wasn't right. When I turned eighteen, at least five years after the sexual acts had stopped, she decided it was time for me to see a psychologist. By then, the abuse had ended, but the damage kept growing year after year.

On my own and without help, I couldn't get out. And even going to therapy was taboo. Just like it still is for many. You don't want anyone to know. If they found out, they'd assume you were crazy or broken. In a small community like ours - 140.000 inhabitants - news travels faster than fire. And the last thing I needed was for people to poke fingers into wounds I was already continuously scratching.

At eighteen, freshly done with school, I couldn't keep handling the way I felt inside. On the outside, I was bubbly, attention-grabbing, bold, and everyone's best friend. Pretending I lacked nothing, suppressing my inner truth. That's how I lived my life.

I didn't feel like myself anymore. I was someone who just... existed. I tried in every way possible to heal myself, or rather, to fill myself up. Furthermore, I became a girl constantly searching for something to fill the emptiness, to numb the pain. Not only that, but I wanted people to see me and recognize me for who I was and not for what had happened to me or who I had become. No one truly saw what was going on inside me.

I drove my car fast, raced against guys, drank, smoked, and lived in a way that had danger written all over it. Self-destructiveness! I would go out and come home at dawn, then sleep until two in the afternoon. Sure, teens like to sleep, but I did it for another reason. I wanted to harm myself. I didn't want to live with myself anymore. I felt torn.

Part of me wanted to know who I really was, even though I didn't know. That part fought with the version of me that was trying to destroy everything I had been before the abuse. It was like a fire burning through me.

The first time my mother took me to the psychologist, I walked in alone. She was a woman, younger than my mother, probably ten years older than me. I guess she was about the same age as my sister. She was short, and something about her presence intrigued me. I felt like I could talk to her without being judged. This was her job. She assured me that everything we discussed would stay between us. That session became the first of many I would attend for years to come. And unaware, she sowed the first seed in me of a passion I would only recognize much later.

How do you talk about something that's been buried inside you for ten years? How do you dig up what's been hidden so deep? How do you bring it to the surface when it fills you with disgust of yourself? How do you betray your family's image, placing that truth on a platform in front of a stranger? We have a saying on the island: "You don't hang your dirty laundry in public." Initially meant figuratively, but in my case, it was literal too.

How do you bring shame on yourself and others? How do you expose everything? Because there comes a time in life when you just can't cover it up anymore. You'll explode if you don't talk to someone you trust. In the end, what's hidden always finds its way to the light. I couldn't stay silent anymore. For the sake of my sanity, silence was no longer an option. I couldn't handle the weight of the situation. I needed help. Desperately.

The wounds were putrefying. I was spitting pus - like venom - onto myself and those around me. It affected how I thought about myself and others. At some point, I decided, I don't know when exactly, that I would talk. I would say everything. Every single thing!

At least I would try to speak and express what I remembered. Because I had suppressed the acts so deeply, I'd forgotten too much. The psychologist encouraged me to share it all with my parents. So, at nineteen, I sat at the table, having invited my parents for a conversation. I told them everything.

We were seated at the dining table. My father at the head. My mother to his right. Sitting beside her, I lowered my head

- ashamed and afraid - I began to speak. Tears poured from the depths of my soul, running down like a river from my eyes. "First the water... the rest follows."

I was consumed by pain, and sadness wrapped itself around me. My lips trembled. My throat closed. My stomach twisted. My legs wouldn't stop shaking. I felt myself fading. My hands were cold. The tears I had held back for so long now poured like a broken dam. They burst free. And carefully choosing what to say to protect myself, to protect my cousin, and to protect my parents, I spoke.

After all that effort, my mother cried and asked if what had happened wasn't just something between kids. She ended with a question: "Do you want me to talk to your cousin or the family?"

"To my cousin or the family?" I answered immediately. No!

Then my father, calm as always, said, "This is what happens. We open our home to help someone, and they abuse our trust. End of conversation."

They never brought it up again.

I didn't know whether to feel relieved or heartbroken. Part of me wanted them to defend me and take action. Another part was glad everything stayed the same. Such a confrontation I could not handle anyway.

For a long time, I blamed them. After all the courage it took for me to speak up, I hadn't expected this response. I felt like they didn't take it seriously, like they left me hanging. Alone and without safety. Even though maybe, for them, this was their way of protecting me, because I was the one who told them not to share the information. Me, naïve as ever.

The relationship between them and my cousin, between my cousin and our family, and our friends, stayed exactly the same. And I was left with nothing but silence. Forced to live as though nothing had ever happened. For years to come.

I AM READY

*My soul hit the ground, and all that
remained
It was a vast, deep silence.
In that silence, I began to reflect,
And through reflection, I realized:
I had to let go.
Because a quiet strength still remained
And that one last beam of light
continued to shine.
I couldn't hold on any longer.
I had to accept reality.
I opened my hands and released it.
And right then, the enormous burden
That weight on my back fell away.
I could finally breathe again*

And feel a freshness, like rain...falling.
Somewhere deep within,
the pain still stirred,
But my heart and mind were
ready to accept
That even in my loss,
I was ready to move on.
Step by step, I would rise again.
And even if I stumbled from time to time,
The One who held my hand
would not let me fall.
I could lean on Him
Because He had already promised
That He would carry me into my old age.
I had found the key! Yes! He is my key.
The One who gave everything just to
save me.

4. THE REST COMES AFTER

Life went on, and I silenced the past. I kept growing, and the little girl became a woman. I studied, went out, kept myself busy with friends, dated, and ran. I ran from Curaçao, from my family, from anyone or anything that reminded me of my past. What I didn't realize was that when I left, I carried a suitcase full of my own baggage. My sadness, my scattered emotions, and the burning smell.

I ran, but I couldn't hide from the truth or the reality. Every family gathering reminded me of the nightmare and that I couldn't bring problems into the family by telling what had happened.

Hiding in the arms of my boyfriend and pretending I had no past worked, until one day, my past brought back memories I really wanted to forget. Filling the emptiness worked temporarily. That constant need to feel full remained. Isn't that how we fill what's empty? At all costs. Even if it means filling it with whatever is needed or available. Life itself held up a mirror and showed me that I wasn't facing the wounds - or rather, the marks - of my past.

The way I dealt with what had happened was by pretending it didn't. Trying to forget the experiences I had. Continuing life, holding up a façade that masked the truth. And I did that for quite a while.

I went on with life and met the man who became my first husband. I told him what had happened in my childhood, though not all the details. I explained why I needed to shower and sometimes cry after we were intimate.

Every sexual moment of intimacy would end with me on the shower floor, crying under the water, hoping it would wash away the dirt of the past. Sitting there, I cried. As if the water could remove the mud for a moment. My tears disappeared into the stream that cleansed my outside, but inside, nothing changed. The pain I felt remained. Still, he accepted me as I was, and for the first time, I had someone who knew what I have been through. I didn't need to hide anything from him. That helped for a long time. But it didn't bring inner peace. I hadn't yet forgiven nor accepted myself.

In 1996, my partner Menno - my child's father - and I moved to the Netherlands. There, we got married. Our life gained stability, and that lifestyle began to satisfy me. I was happy with what we were building. A home, our first jobs, and the steps I was beginning to take toward studying again. I didn't need to attend any family events or see anyone from back home. My husband's family became mine, and that felt good.

I built walls around myself that kept others out and surrounded myself with people who knew nothing about my past. I felt comfortable in my own skin because I had "forgotten." The frequent handwashing and long showers became normal. But now I wasn't even thinking about it. It had just become routine. Nothing more than habit. My husband and child filled my life enough.

"Alles went" everything adjusts, as the Dutch say. I had found a way to deal with my situation, and I liked it. At home, in my personal life, socially, as a volunteer, and in my career, my focus was always on others. Taking care of others, being attentive to others, dedicating and committing myself to others so I wouldn't have to face myself. That's how I kept filling the void left by the many wounds of my youth. Because remember... Giving is better than receiving! That's what my parents taught me when they took my cousin into our home. I became the light that used to shine through the hallway into the room! This time, my light was meant for others. The one who helps, the one who gives and spreads warmth where shadows lingered. Even though my own inner room remained in darkness. Life was good, and I wanted to keep it that way. Why wake something up that's finally asleep?

But life has a way of revealing itself, sometimes leaving you completely exposed. In the year 2000, Menno, our child, and I traveled to Curaçao on vacation. We had done so almost every year. As the plane landed, my body relaxed in a way I hadn't felt in years. The tropical wind touched my face, and I inhaled deeply. The bright colors caressed my eyes, dull from months of winter. I was finally home. again..

But that vacation was different. One day, while driving through the neighborhood of Saliña, we got a little lost and ended up in a side alley. There, we came upon a dead-end street, and I saw it.

Right in front of me stood a tree that looked exactly like the one that had symbolized my childhood. The tree of my youth. The tree of my innocence. The one where I had lived my sweet days. The flamboyant tree, standing tall. Large, with strong branches, ready to carry me now with all my baggage. So similar as the tree I had swung from and sat in for hours. Its scent swept under my nose and reopened all my senses.

Suddenly, I was back. Back in that precious time, and with it, everything came flooding in. Not just the good memories. I could hear my Nana's voice echoing again. But I was also back in that room. Back on the floor. Back under the weight. Once again, the bitterness touches my lips. The sting of past pain pressed in again. Scars I'd buried now lit with a flame I never meant to feel again.

In a blink, I was back in that room, lying on the floor. My senses are on high alert. Doing what had been expected, what had become routine. I saw the light again... under the door... but no one was coming. I was back in that space and reliving those moments - again - only years later. Consumed by flames but not the kind that purifies or sanctifies. No, this was the fire of destruction.

The same cards were on the table. Which one would I play? What now, with everything resurfacing? Would I push the thoughts and feelings away again? Or would I finally confront them and deal with them?

This time, I spoke to my husband about it, deeper than ever before. I shared the details. One in particular filled me with shame. Retelling those moments made me want to throw up. My stomach turned. I wanted to strip away everything I carried inside. Shame screamed within me. Disgust. Filth. "I want to die!".

I told my husband what had stirred it all up; how just seeing the flamboyant tree had set it in motion. His eyes filled with tears. He stopped the car. We talked. And I decided I wanted to confront my cousin.

From my mother, I learned that my cousin now had a daughter. My first thought was: Now that he has a little girl, maybe he'll realize what he did to someone else's daughter.

We planned a visit to meet the newborn. Me, my husband, and our daughter went. Sitting in the car, I looked in the rearview mirror and saw my daughter in the back seat. Singing. Playing with her Barbie. Smiling. Dancing to her own song. The wind in her hair. She pulled a few strands from her eyes. Her eyes met mine in the mirror. Innocence. She had no idea about the visit we were about to make. And I... I saw myself in her.

With steady steps, I walked toward the front door. I felt my husband's hand touching me lightly in my back. My heart was pounding in my throat. The same wind, now kissed my face, drying the tears welling in my eyes. I brushed them off with trembling fingers, dabbing them quietly onto my clothes.

As we stepped inside, my heart's beating now louder and heavier. The closer we got, the deeper I breathed. My hands were sweaty. We went in. Before I could even take in the house, we followed Carlos - my cousin - to his newborn baby. I felt like I was losing my breath. I was drowning.

We admired the baby girl's beauty. We didn't stay long. As we said goodbye, I asked if I could speak to him outside for a moment.

My husband, who already knew what I was about to do, took our daughter to the car to wait.

I asked my cousin if he remembered what had happened when I was little. I told him how much pain and damage it had caused me. How it had shaped and misshaped me. How I had struggled even to the point that I couldn't have a healthy intimate relationship with my husband. I told him I forgave him. He listened for a long time, without interrupting. Then he lowered his head, looked me in the eye, and said he hadn't forgotten. He could not! Not a day went by where he didn't think about it. That he never meant to hurt me, and he asked me to forgive him.

I told him again that I forgave him. I hoped he would enjoy his daughter and be a good father to her. I gave him a hug and walked to the car where my husband and child were waiting. As soon as I got in, my husband started the car and drove toward my parents' house.

He asked, "How did it go?"

And without words, I burst into tears.

A river flowed from the depths of my stomach. I cried for all the years. I cried for my childhood, my youth, my dreams, my values. I cried for the pain and rage I felt toward myself and toward him. I cried all the tears I had once cried in the shower. I let out a scream for all the years I had stayed silent, pretending everything was okay.

Those tears washed away the dirt of my past, this time not only on the outside, but also from within. They removed the filth from my mind, my body, my soul, releasing me from guilt, shame, fear, resentment, and rage. So much rage, because I didn't know who I was. I had lost my own identity and dignity. All my trust in myself and in others had been stripped away.

What I had learned in church - what God had said and shown me - I put into practice. Could forgiveness truly set me free?

At the very least, I had taken the first step making room for healing to begin.

Sometimes, I still wish my parents had reacted differently. That they had known how to handle the situation. That they had talked openly and gone deeper. Maybe it would have been better if they hadn't tried to protect me but had confronted my cousin and exposed it to the family. Maybe then I wouldn't have felt like a child that was told: "It happened, now get up and go play."

Yes, protecting family and keeping peace is important. But at what cost? They might've also wondered how I could bring this up after ten years. What were they supposed to do after so long?

Life had moved on... even if fear, shame, and insecurity had kept me silent for so long.

Still, I came to understand their side too.

As a child, my parents taught me - directly or indirectly - that I had to listen to those older than me. I was raised to "eat everything on my plate," even what didn't taste good. I was expected to obey without questioning, or I'd be labeled disrespectful. I had to call strangers 'aunt' and 'uncle.' That meant my cousin should have known better. He should have protected me. And all of those unspoken expectations played a role - consciously or unconsciously - in keeping everything buried.

How must my father have felt? His daughter went through something like this. As a man, he hadn't been able to protect me. The guilt rested on all of our shoulders.

Blaming someone is a hard question to answer.

We each had to deal with it in our own way.

After that vacation, the process of forgiveness truly began. But how do you forgive something like that? The unforgivable...

I had to take the steps to forgive my cousin for his ignorance and to forgive myself.

For the first time, I could see it wasn't my fault.

I hadn't done anything to provoke him.

I forgave myself for not asking for help sooner.

For not speaking up earlier.

For the times I hurt others in my pain.

For the times I sought sexual satisfaction alone, in the shower.

Because in the end, the very thing I detested had become part of me.

I forgave myself for the anger I felt toward black men in general.

I forgave my mother and father for not knowing how to respond.

I forgave my siblings because they didn't know, they could have not known.

Back then, protection had become impossible.

I faced the truth: I was angry with God for not intervening when I needed Him most. And finally, I forgave myself for feeling that way for so long.

After years of processing, I reached acceptance of the scars left behind when the wounds finally healed.

But forgiveness didn't happen overnight. The desire was there, but it took years before I truly felt I had forgiven myself and those involved. It was a process. Sometimes, I had to remind myself daily.

But I know this: choosing to forgive set me free.

It broke the chains tying me to that moment.

It meant I had to tell myself that I wasn't at fault.

That everything that happened had a reason, a purpose?

Staying angry and living in pain wouldn't change what happened, but it would keep me imprisoned by it.

Letting go didn't erase the past, but it stopped it from having power over me.

Forgiveness, like many things in life, is a choice. It doesn't happen on its own. Without God's help, it would've been impossible.

I didn't choose for those things to happen to me, but I do choose how I respond to them.

I had to work every day to treat those around me with love - instead of bleeding continuously on them - even when I didn't feel like it.

Most days, I wanted to fall back into victimhood. Most days, I wanted to go back to the feeling that had trapped me for so long. But I had to rise each day and decide again to face it all.Despite what had happened or what hadn't. I couldn't stay stuck in what others did or didn't do.

We all, in some way, contributed, knowingly or unknowingly. I had to process what happened on every level: mentally, emotionally, spiritually, and through every choice moving forward.

Now, when I look back or when someone talks to me about sexual abuse, I feel compassion. I understand, to some degree, what they may feel or be going through. I'm ready to listen without letting past pain overwhelm me. I no longer project my story onto theirs. I can speak on the topic without crying or reliving it all again.

I used to be unable to sleep unless a light from outside was shining into my room. I couldn't sleep on the side of the bed closest to the door or near a window. I was afraid of who might come in. Even as an adult, I always slept against the wall. It gave me a sense of safety.

I couldn't be emotionally present during intimacy. I couldn't be with a man of my own skin color.

I couldn't satisfy my partner sexually through oral sex. Sex felt dirty, not beautiful. I couldn't see myself as a worthy woman, but rather, a used one. My self-image and sense of worth were shattered, and it blocked my confidence. I became a woman who focused entirely on the needs of others and my career, because deep down, I didn't see myself as someone who had a right to simply exist.

All of that - after more than thirty years is now a scar. A mark on my skin, no longer a wound in my soul. Those wounds are healed. Restored! They are a chapter in my life, but no longer my whole story. The survival strategies that once kept me safe have outlived their purpose; I no longer need to bleed in silence to feel safe.

Because now, I am living.

Now, I use what happened as a weapon to shape, uplift, counsel, listen to others, and rebuild.

I've come to understand that everything I've lived through is a powerful tool.

That's what it means to take what came to destroy you and use it for good. To me, it's no longer a taboo. I am not the first, and I won't be the last to go through this kind of experience.

But how we each rise from it that's what makes the difference.

Yes, it's hard... but no. It's not impossible.

Today, I have a positive image of myself.

I've regained my self-confidence. The marks left behind are mine, they belong to me.

They helped shape who I am today. I could never be who I am now without them.

So I've chosen to embrace what they represent: *Me!*

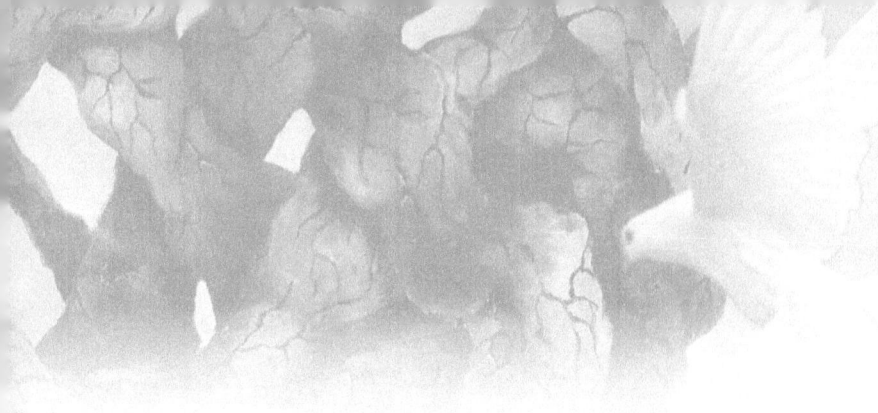

YOUR PLACE

When you're tired and fed up,
When discomfort overwhelms you,
When anger rises and you don't know how
to express it,
When disappointment grips your chest,
When your joy has been stolen,
When your peace has disappeared and you
don't know where to find it—

I want to encourage you not to give up.
I've found you a powerful place.
The journey there costs nothing.
You don't have to pay a thing, just show up,
and you'll be transformed.
Your stay has no limit. You can remain as

long as you need.
Are you ready? Because your journey
begins now.

Aha! you want to know the name of
the place?
Its name is: The arms of your Lord.

There, love overflows.
Peace is abundant.
Joy returns.
Comfort and forgiveness will be your
nourishment.
It won't be long before you receive
renewed strength
So you'll be ready to face whatever lies
ahead on your path.

Now, are you ready?
Alright! Let the journey begin.

5. IDENTITY

It's not easy to grow up in a place where people are treated differently based on the color of their skin, the texture of their hair, their last name, their neighborhood, the school they attend, or their family's financial status.

Many times, we ourselves treat people with names like Perreira, Diaz, Van de... or Van der... differently than we treat those with the last name Zimmerman or Cijntje.

We talk about "good hair" and "bad hair." Kids we call "white" here because of their lighter skin or fine hair, in the Netherlands are labeled "allochtonen" - people with a migration background - and compared to Turks or Moroccans which were not that welcome either.

What I later realized was that even in the Netherlands, I had to deal with the same kinds of distinctions and discrimination, between white and Black, light skin and dark skin, fine hair and coarse, and families with status versus those without.

I had all kinds of friends who weren't defined by one background, but when I look back now, there were still small social groups: Portuguese, Dutch-Europeans, Black Curaçaoans, and Black Curaçaoans from "good" (wealthy) families. Then there were those who were Black but wished they were white - the so - called "Black Makambas."

And yes, in Curaçao, we even used the word "kaffers" (deeply racist and unacceptable). A sad but true reality.

We were Black kids from Curaçao, with coarse hair, a family from Westpunt, living in Mahaai. We grew up in a large house with hardworking parents who had money. We went to a school attended mostly by "white" children, and we loved it!

All I have are good memories of that school. Sweet times! Teachers who were passionate and dedicated.

My parents wanted us in a good school, so they sent us to "Albert Schweitzer College" for both primary and secondary education. That school had a good reputation in those days. There were many white children, lighter-skinned children, and dark-skinned children whose parents had deliberately chosen to send them to a quality school.

To attend "Albert Schweitzer College", you had to live in the right area or be Protestant. We were neither. We lived in "Mahaai", a neighbourhood who was not in the area and were Catholic. Still, we went to that school. And we were proud of it. Maybe we had a godparent- sponsor or someone who helped us to get in...

When I finished Albert Schweitzer College, I left for the Netherlands. That was during a time of big changes in the education system. Suddenly there were a lot of issues, and my parents became worried about my future development in Curaçao. I loved learning, and they didn't want my education to be compromised.

So I couldn't wait to leave. And at just sixteen years old, I moved to the Netherlands to live with a Dutch-European family who were friends of my parents.

To understand how I ended up in certain relationships later, you need to know where I came from.

At sixteen, in the middle of puberty, I was wrestling with my identity, trying to figure out who I was and I moved far away from my parents for the first time. I went to live in a small town with a Dutch family. Back then, the only non-white family in that entire town was a Chinese family who owned the local Chinese restaurant.

There were no Black people there. Not even dark-skinned individuals with curly hair. Even the Chinese were considered dark enough.

While many students went to big cities like Rotterdam, Amsterdam, The Hague, or Tilburg to study, I ended up hearing Dutch teens asking, "Can Black skin come off?" when they saw someone like me.

I remember where I lived - a village called Mijnsheerenland in the Hoeksche Waard region near Rotterdam.

That's where I experienced hailstones for the first time. I actually thought someone was throwing ice at me.

Once on a bus, a boy sitting next to me asked if my skin tasted like chocolate.

At school, someone asked me what I had done to my hair to make it grow so fast, because I had come to school one day with short hair and the next with long braids that a fellow Curaçaoan girl had installed.

I lived with that family for a year, but eventually, I couldn't handle the homesickness.

Back then, a phone call to Curaçao cost a lot, so you could only call once or twice a week. When I did, my mom and I would shout on the phone like we couldn't hear each other, because of the distance.

That year, at a crucial point in my growth, something in me cracked open and changed forever. I took in so many things from that Dutch family: neighborhood habits, European customs. Their way of thinking, dressing, speaking, and acting.

In the Netherlands, they thought it was great how quickly I adapted. But when I returned to Curaçao, my family and people around me didn't like it at all. I came back the same Black girl with coarse hair but with a "white mentality". My style of dress and behavior resembled that of white people.

When I resumed my studies at MIL, people tried to label me as a "Black Makamba" or an Oreo cookie. Only a small group accepted me.

One teacher even kicked me out of class for asking a question they thought was inappropriate for a student to ask a teacher. In the Netherlands, I had been told to speak up and ask critical questions. I had gone to the Netherlands one way and returned another.

Many times, other Curaçaoan youth didn't accept me. The local boys didn't like how I was either.

But Dutch men at the time were fascinated by young Caribbean women who looked like me. Caribbean appearance, Western thinking, fluent in Dutch.

I always dreamed that one day I'd meet the prince who would make me his princess. Ever since I was a child reading fairy tales, I was fascinated by anything to do with love. The stories I read and watched on TV filled me with hope for a bright future.

Who doesn't know that fluttery feeling in your stomach that makes your heart race? Blood rushing through your body. Sometimes it's a warm sensation, other times cold. Either way, my hands would get sweaty. Love itself - and love for a man - was normal and natural to me.

I was raised in a family where my mom and dad, in my eyes, were happily married. I saw that as a blessing. I longed for the day I'd share my life with someone. That longing to live out my own fairy tale made me too eager at times.

Every relationship I had, I thought would end in marriage. But none did. I lacked patience. I often moved faster than the other person and didn't give the relationship the time it needed to grow into something stable. The pressure I put on myself and my partners wasn't healthy. My way of attaching to people drained them and broke down whatever we had built.

I met the man who would become my husband when I was nineteen and he was eighteen.

I never thought we'd end up together. I didn't even like younger or shorter men. And he was both.

At the time, I was running a small modeling agency called 'Go Diva'. Not full-time, but I used my experience with the runway and dance to train models and choreograph their routines.

He was one of those models. We practiced on weekends. He was dating a girl I thought was perfect for him. In my eyes, they were a great match. I wasn't interested in him, and he wasn't interested in me.

He had an athletic body and was a couple of centimeters shorter than me. His hair was long, with big curls that fell past his shoulders, all the way down his muscled back. His eyes were hazel and wide, mysterious. His skin tone matched his eye color. When the sun hit his bronzed skin, it glowed like copper touched with a hint of gold. With defined cheekbones and fine lips...

But what really captured me was that his jawline reminded me of Brad Pitt.

His hair was dark, but the sun gave it golden highlights. His look was more surfer, though he didn't surf. His life revolved around the ocean, and eventually, he found his passion working with sea animals.

His appearance was a mix of white European and Indonesian features. Specifically, he was 75% Dutch-European and 25% Indonesian. His father was Dutch with German and Swedish roots. His mother was half Dutch-European and half Indonesian-Chinese.

They had lived in Curaçao for a few years.

At the time, I was a nineteen-year-old Afro-Caribbean girl, 1.78 meters tall, with beautiful curves and coiled hair. And I was fully aware that a white man was attracted to me.

Back then, marines would visit Curaçao and were often fascinated by Caribbean women. But he fell into a different category of man. Even his girlfriend had the same features as him, curly light hair and light skin.

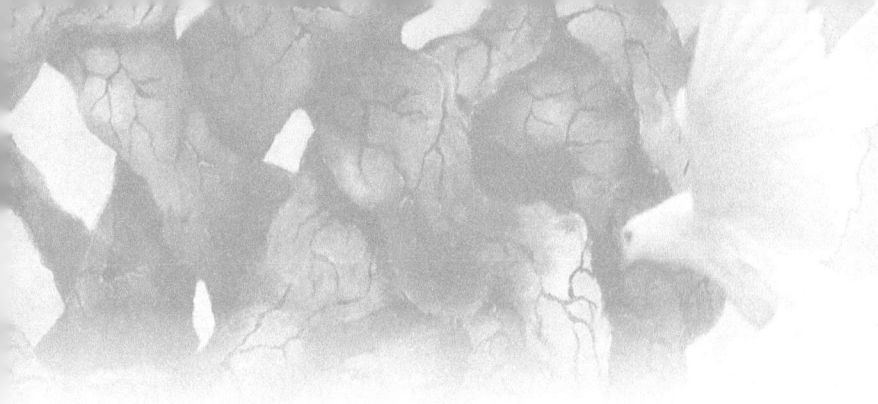

TEARS

Tears in my eyes... Where are you?
It's been so long since you left me behind.
In every corner, every crack, I search for
you in desperation.
But it seems you've run away and
can't be found.
It feels like a dam is breaking,
And the pressure bends the steel.
If it lasts much longer,
My heart will explode.

My mouth refuses to open.
The words won't come out.
You are my only escape,
My only way to express

What I am carrying inside.

Oh Lord, my God,
Come to my aid.
I've read in Your Word
That You catch every tear that falls,
Because it's through them
That You understand
What my mouth cannot speak.

Oh Lord, my God,
Come to my aid.
I don't want my soul to give out.
Before You, I confess,
Because I want to be set free
So that healing can begin.

When you feel tired and worn out,
When discomfort gets under your skin,
When anger bubbles up and you don't
know how to release it,
When disappointment floods your chest,
When your joy has been stolen,
When your peace has disappeared and you

don't know where to find it
I want to encourage you: do not despair.

I've found you a powerful place.
The journey to get there is free.
You don't need to pay, just show up, and
transformation will meet you there.
There's no limit to your stay. Stay as long
as you need.

Ready? Your journey starts now.
You want to know the name of this place?
Its name is: The arms of your Lord.
There, love is abundant.
Peace flows freely.
Joy that was missing is restored.
Comfort and forgiveness will nourish you.
And soon, you'll receive renewed strength,
So that you are equipped to face
Everything your path brings your way.

Now, are you ready?
Let the journey begin.

6. ACCEPTANCE?

In my search to understand who I was - struggling with identity and self-acceptance - I ended up in a close friendship with this handsome young man. We often met at the gym and talked a lot. Through mutual friends, we started seeing each other more and gradually became closer.

What I appreciated most about our bond was that we could just be ourselves. Because there were no expectations, we were relaxed, open, and could talk about everything. He told me about his breakup with his girlfriend, and in our own ways, we supported each other during that time. We visited each other's homes frequently, our parents knew each other, and we hung out a lot, watching movies, going out, drinking, smoking, playing cards, and talking about life.

We became what you would now call BFs, best friends. We trusted each other deeply and shared everything. It reached a point where it felt like we were against the world together. We even helped each other meet potential partners and talked about our dreams for the future. When the modeling project at Go Diva ended, I started working temporarily in the hospitality industry. There were times when we worked behind the bar together and lived a seemingly perfect life.

My mother always told me never to date my best friend. She warned me that if the relationship didn't work out, I'd lose a good friend forever. I heard her, but I didn't listen. Maybe we confused our friendship for romantic love. But we ended up together.

On one perfect night, after dinner with his family, he kissed me, and I kissed him back... and just like that, our fate was sealed. Everything moved quickly. His parents didn't approve of the relationship, and he decided to move out.

Since I had already been living semi-independently, I welcomed him into my studio apartment. Fueled by rebellion and love, we moved in together without our parents' blessing. At the time, we didn't realize the seriousness or implications of our decision. It was joy without caution, togetherness without fear. Just us, and that was enough.

His father made it clear that I was no longer welcome at their home, not even to park in their street. That only pushed his son further away. Soon after, he packed his bags and left. We were young and naïve, heading into a battle we couldn't win. Despite everything, we believed nothing and no one could separate us.

That same year, he was twenty and I was twenty-one, I got pregnant. I remember lying on a mattress with him while Caminando Por la Calle by the Gipsy Kings played in the background. I turned to him and said, "If we sleep together unprotected, I could get pregnant." But with hearts and flesh stirred by untamed hunger neither of us said or did anything to stop it. Two months later, I found out I was pregnant.

We moved near my parents and started a new life. Despite growing up in a family where everything was provided - maid and nannie- included - my mother always taught me that a woman takes care of her home. That's what I wanted. Despite my young age, I wanted to be a good woman and a good mother. I was ready to build a family.

I had dropped out of senior year in high school a few years earlier, and my partner had finished secondary school two years prior. We were both working, and things with his parents eventually calmed down. My parents supported us. When our daughter was born, she brought light and joy into our lives.

Getting pregnant awakened a deep need in me for something greater. Life wasn't easy, and the only place I knew to go for what I needed was to God. That's exactly what I did. I rededicated my life to God and decided to live a life of faith and trust in Him.

When our daughter turned one, we moved back to the Netherlands. We weren't satisfied. Neither of us had finished school. We were both working for minimum wage and didn't see a solid future. We wanted more for our daughter.

His parents had returned to the Netherlands before us and offered to support us if we came back to study. So we moved and started over, staying with his grandmother in the heart of Amsterdam. Our plan was to work and study to build a better future.

At first, things seemed promising. But soon, obstacles began to interfere. I worked in hospitality, and he picked up various jobs. While we were at work, his family cared for our daughter. They supported us.

But living with family in someone else's home isn't easy. Tensions grew. Our cultures clashed. Soon, I no longer felt at home. One weekend, while I was out having dinner with a friend, my partner called me on the train back. He said I couldn't come home. His grandmother no longer wanted me there.

A cold chill ran through me. My eyes could have shot out fire from the rage. Why won't they stop? Where am I supposed to go now? What did I do wrong, again?

To this day, I don't know what triggered his grandmother's sudden decision. She told him only he and the baby could stay. But for the second time, he stood up for us both. He decided that neither of us would stay. It was

Christmas Eve 1996. We'd only been in the Netherlands for four months.

He asked his parents to keep the baby for a night while we figured things out. The next day, when we had a plan, we would go get her. So he met me at the train station. We woke on Christmas Day with no home, no sense of where to go.

The cold winter wind slapped my face while my tears failed to do their job. Where would we go? The station was packed, yet we were all alone. I tried to hold back my tears, but my heart raced. I didn't know if I felt anger or sadness or both. I couldn't stand the cold.

We looked at each other. I saw the sorrow and desperation in his eyes. But at that moment, I couldn't feel anything. Nothing made sense. I wanted to blame someone, but I didn't know who. Wasn't it me who got pregnant?

There we stood at Amsterdam Central Station. It felt like a bad dream.

We couldn't return to Curaçao. We had nowhere to go in the Netherlands. And for the first time, without many words, we began to blame each other. The feelings of powerlessness, failure, rejection, it all came over us.

It was just past midnight. Christmas Sunday. The middle of winter. How could I forget such a painful moment? I knew if I called my parents, they'd tell me, "Come home, my child." They would've done everything in their power to bring us home. But I didn't want to.

We didn't want to. We were tired of running, tired of fighting, tired of struggling with no progress. We didn't want to give them bad news. That would mean we'd accepted defeat and we couldn't.

So I called a friend - an ex-girlfriend of my brother - who lived in Amsterdam Southeast. She opened her home to us immediately. She picked us up from the station. It was a small two-bedroom apartment on the third floor in

Heesterveld.

The next day, he went to pick up our daughter and brought her to stay with us. We lived there for months. For at least a year, I had no contact with his family. He and the baby visited them weekly, but the pain of their rejection and lack of acceptance was embedded in my soul. I later realized they never truly accepted me.

They once said he should have been with a Javanese woman. Naïve as I was, I believed I didn't need their approval to be with the man I loved. But deep down, their acceptance - and the acceptance of others - mattered more than I admitted. I lost myself without realizing it. My dream of belonging to a complete family, on both sides, never materialized. Even in the Netherlands, I was far from my own family and pushed aside by his family. I felt like a stranger, neglected, rejected once again. A failure.

Time passed. Eventually, his family relationship improved. We visited every weekend and even took vacations with them. But the seed of rejection had taken root. It grew into a tree bearing bitter fruit; fruit neither of us wanted to eat.

After that dark Christmas night in 1996, our lives took another turn. My friend's family embraced and supported us. They made us feel like family. We shared everything. But despite that, my wounds and memories weighed heavily. I loved him and our daughter deeply, but I struggled with the past.

My pain resurfaced like a flood. I felt worthless, not good enough, useless. It was as if a cloud hovered over me, even in the midst of blessings. A deep loneliness overwhelmed me. I felt alone in my own family, in groups of people. Even when I had what I thought I wanted.

I realized I wasn't truly living. My sister advised me to visit a church in Amsterdam Southeast, the same one I used to attend in Curaçao. I remember going there with my partner and our daughter. The services were held in a small community center in Reigersbos.

As we walked in, I felt something shift. I remember it like it was yesterday. The people were joyful, singing about joy, hope, healing, and salvation. They sang in Papiamentu - my native language - too, and there were many people from Curaçao. The music was gospel infused with salsa, merengue, and tumba. Even in the cold, the place radiated warmth. I felt like I had arrived, like this was where I was supposed to be.

They sang with us, embraced us, looked into our eyes with love. It was divine acceptance. I wanted what they had, whatever made them glow from within.

The music slowed. A woman began to sing gently. Her words were profound: "As the deer pants for the water, so my soul longs for You." Words from Psalm

42:1. I sang with everything in me. I longed for my soul to find relief. I began to cry, tears poured down uncontrollably.

It felt like something inside me broke. They kept singing for at least thirty more minutes, and my tears didn't stop. I kept trying to wipe them away. Then I felt something strange. My tears felt thick. like oil in my hands. The sensation was soft, like velvet. I felt transported. Everything around me disappeared. Just as I felt like I was leaving, I opened my eyes in fear... and the oily tears slid from my hands. My partner's eyes were red too. He'd received his portion as well.

That day marked a new beginning.

To this day, I don't know exactly what it was, but God gave it a deeper meaning. I experienced something supernatural and felt His presence. Even if I didn't understand it then, I knew something had shifted.

We began attending church weekly. We received hope and strength. We became part of that community. On Sundays we heard the Word, on Tuesdays we prayed, and on Fridays we studied the Bible. We were hungry for God and His truth. We wanted to know Him and be more like Him.

We tried to live according to what we were learning. No one forced us. We simply chose to obey God. The pastor preached about living together and how it wasn't pleasing to God. So we quickly decided to focus on marriage. They advised us to live apart while preparing to marry. He stayed with a Christian brother, and I with a Christian sister. We wanted to please God.

In our pain, we called on God. In our poverty, we trusted Him for provision. We gave our offerings, raised our daughter in God's ways, and were grateful. Our way of dressing, speaking, and living changed. We did everything for our salvation; to avoid ending up in hell!

Little by little, we distanced ourselves from what they called "worldly" influences. We threw away "worldly" music, stopped listening to secular radio, stopped sleeping together without being married, and sold items deemed unholy. We stopped drinking and smoking to live a holy life.

Not every show was fit to watch, and not every book fit to read. We did all that. Later, as youth leaders, we taught others the same, despite the consequences. All we wanted was to be loved by God. To be saved. To be accepted.

I remember the sister who took me in. Looking back, she was deeply religious. Everything began and ended with prayer, fasting, and speaking in tongues. Everything was "in the blood of Jesus" or "in Jesus' name." She was a single mother struggling with her children. Life wasn't easy, but she held on to God. She always declared she was blessed. She modeled that for me.

One night, I lay in bed with our daughter beside me. She was about a year and a half old. The room was small, dark, cluttered with sacks and boxes, barely enough space to move. I could hear rats or something huge scurrying in the walls.

Our bed sagged like a hammock. The springs poked my back. No matter how I turned, I couldn't get comfortable. How did I end up here? Me, who had everything. How did I get to this place? I looked around but saw nothing. The room seemed darker. The shadows became people. The walls closed in. My stomach turned. My forehead dripped sweat, though no water leaked.

Fear took over. My thoughts spiraled. How did I get here? I missed my partner, my parents, and a joyful life. I held our daughter closer. Then I saw a window. In all the darkness, there was a window. There was a way out. There was light.

I lifted my eyes and, for the first time, deeply and truly, I thanked God.

Thanked Him for all that had happened and was still happening. And strangely enough... Not long after that day, we got engaged.

No! Our wedding was nothing like the one I dreamed of as a girl. We got married in July 1997. My mom and dad flew in from Curaçao so my dad could walk me down the aisle. My husband's parents and siblings, though invited, didn't come. Everyone from our church showed up. They put their hands and hearts to work and made the wedding possible. We had no money to do anything ourselves.

My dress was second-hand. I bought it for 200 guilders in a thrift shop in Amsterdam. Some of the church women helped me take it to a seamstress to make it more my style. At the time, we had only 500 guilders to cover the reception. Friends and church family helped with everything. Thanks to them, we had food and drinks for all our guests. They took our wedding pictures with disposable cameras.

The ceremony was held in the community center that the church was renting back then. We couldn't afford wedding rings, so we used the friendship rings we already had from our time together in Curaçao. Our cake and buffet were also gifts. Both of us were dressed in white with pearl and ice tones, and our wedding theme was sunflowers. My dad gave me away, and our daughter carried our rings. None of the material things mattered. What mattered was that we were finally married. That we could finally be together. That we could continue our lives together, in a sacred union, in the eyes of God. That's all we wanted: to be together - at last - as a family.

Whether everything we did - or didn't do - was right or wrong, one thing was sure: God provided for us. We found a house in Almere. After six months of sleeping through winter on a mattress (all three of us) directly on a cement floor, we received a fridge, stove, linoleum, and almost everything else we needed from people around us, without even asking.

They would come and ask what we were missing, and then they would bring exactly that. Little by little, we built our home.

Not long after our wedding, my husband received an invitation to the wedding of an old friend from his youth. We decided to go, knowing that we would see his parents again. It would be their first time seeing him and our daughter since they skipped our wedding. For me, it would be the first time seeing them in about a year, without any contact.

We prepared ourselves. No matter what had happened, we were committed to showing love. We walked in glowing, joyful, with our daughter shining like a beam of light, clarity, and hope. We radiated differently, not just in appearance but from within. It was something from the heart.

We entered the room and greeted everyone as if nothing had ever happened. The venue had a warm, Christmas-like atmosphere. Golden lighting. Velvet chairs. Draped curtains. The light reflecting off the room eased my nerves. We came with hearts willing to forgive. We came so that everyone could experience the love of God now alive in us too.

The following week, his parents invited us over. That became every weekend. And just like that, without ever speaking a single word about what had happened in the past - without ever addressing their absence at our wedding - life went on. Everything returned to "normal."

But what we didn't realize then was that unspoken pain tends to linger.

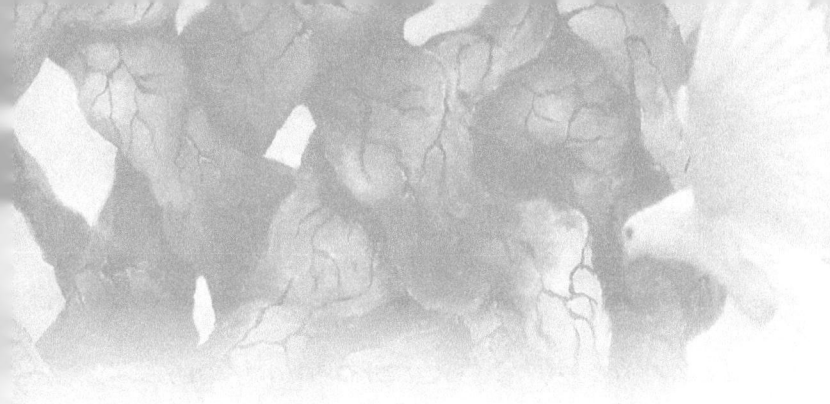

LETTING GO....

Why do you keep looking back,
If what has already happened
Is something that cannot be changed?
Why do you keep insisting,
If what was lost
Can never be returned?
Why do you keep lamenting,
If what wasn't done
Can no longer be accomplished?

Why not repent and accept forgiveness?
Why not forgive the other
And forgive yourself too?

Then take courage, strength, and resolve,
And draw near to the One
Who truly knows your heart.

Let go...
Learn from the failures behind you,
And push yourself forward,
So you can reach meaningful heights.
Fix your eyes and your heart on Him.
Face each day knowing it is a gift from Him,
Because each day is a new opportunity
To reach your goals
And finally fulfil your mission.

That is the reason you were created
To become exactly who God intends
you to be.

7. SEPARATION

The time came when I went back to school and began my study at the University of Applied Sciences in Amsterdam. My husband had worked for a few years at a bank and then found a job at an animal park. Our daughter went to school, and we lived as a stable family. My husband was the head of the household, the man of the house, and I was the woman of the house. We both worked. I was studying alongside, and our daughter knew that everything revolved around her.

For a while, I lived my fairytale.

I loved to cook, and our daughter and I would set the table every evening, waiting for Daddy to come home from work. My husband would do the laundry while I prepared his lunch for the next day. We did the laundry together, ironed together. I cleaned the house and made sure we always had tea or hot chocolate at night so we could enjoy quality time as a family.

We loved to serve and were an example to many. We entertained friends and dedicated our lives to serving God and our church. Our main focus was our family, church, and work. And before we realized it, our lives began to move around church, our daughter, work, and studying - until eventually - our marriage became last on the list.

Our lives continued to concentrate on church and everything related to it. We stopped doing things together and started doing things for the church. Our home was always open to people or families who had no place to stay. Young people who needed a weekend away from their single mothers found a safe home with us. We truly enjoyed this.

Our lives took on new meaning and a deeper dimension. We helped and served others. In our desire to serve God, we began serving people. Church meetings and activities consumed all the time we had left after work and studying. For a long time, we were okay with that. Dedicating our lives more to church activities and the responsibilities that came with it, than to God. We stopped nurturing our relationship. We stopped going out and doing fun things as a couple. We served outside, but our own relationship began to lose its spark.

Whenever we wanted to do or not do something, we would ask the pastor. Only the pastor could speak on God's behalf. Things at church began to go from bad to worse. We started reading other books, watching different sermons, visiting other churches, and eventually concluded that we were in an unhealthy, cult-like environment. When we started asking questions and opening our eyes to what was happening, we were told we were rebellious and needed discipline. That meant we had to stop everything we were doing at church, and those who used to call us "brother and sister" began treating us differently. We had to try to figure out what "sin" we had supposedly committed.

In the years that followed, after being married for just three years, our relationship with my husband's family stabilized, but within the church, slowly but surely, a storm was coming. We eventually experienced a breakdown in the church: adultery among the leaders, people leaving the church in an exodus. Fights for position and recognition. The mother church sent new pastors to support the community, but in the end, it didn't work, and the pastors we knew left. Many divorces followed, with growing distrust and instability. The new pastors had to deal with that. Alongside those events, our marriage also began to deteriorate.

We sought help from professionals specializing in marriage and burnout because, in the meantime, I had been diagnosed with Pfeiffer's disease, which led to a burnout. We even sold our home and moved to another city to receive help. We struggled spiritually. Was it God, the church, or us? We no longer knew what was real. And now we were fighting for our marriage too. We had lost ourselves and each other in the process. Yet we continued to care for our daughter, work, and study as if nothing was wrong. We thought we'd come out stronger and wiser... or so we believed.

All those turbulent events shook the very foundation we thought was so solid. As a couple, we did not survive. Clearly, it was never solid. This entire rollercoaster culminated one night in the second week of November 2004.

Our daughter and I were doing what we did every night. I had cooked, and together we set the table, expecting my husband to arrive around 6 p.m. to eat together. He came in, hung up his jacket, put down his bag, took off his shoes, and walked into the living room like usual. Our daughter ran to him, and he lifted her into the air while I watched them proudly.

He set her down, and she ran upstairs to get something she had made at school for her dad. While she was upstairs, my husband and I sat down at the dining table to eat. As soon as we sat, he lowered his head and said quietly in Dutch,

"I'm going to leave you today."

I replied,

"What did you just say?"

He looked up and repeated,

"I'm going to leave you today."

Silence. I had heard the words, but I couldn't comprehend them.

Right at that moment, our daughter came running down and jumped onto the chair next to me. She looked at both of us. Her first reaction:

"Mom, what happened?"

Then, seeing our silence, she looked at her dad:

"Dad, what happened to Mom?"

And her father replied,

"I'm going to leave Mom."

The only sound I remember after that was our daughter dropping her knife and fork, which I hadn't even noticed she was holding: Tangalangalang!!

Then she asked,

"Where are you going?"

And the reply was:

"To my parents."

Then my husband stood up, we hadn't even eaten, and went upstairs. Our daughter followed him, asking,

"Dad, can I come with you?"

I didn't hear anything else. I remained seated, frozen in my chair.

After a while, I heard him come back down the stairs, our daughter behind him. He had a small suitcase in his hand. He looked at me, said goodbye, and walked out.

Our daughter, who had been one of the few kids in her class with both parents together, now became one of the many children raised without both parents in the home. She was nine years old.

What I experienced after that was a mix of questions and disbelief at what had just happened. That same June, I had completed one of my degree programs, and I was a year away from finishing the second. Just a short time earlier, my husband had shared with me his hope that once I finished university, we would try to have more children. As a family, we had even been praying about it.

Only a few days before it all happened, he had lovingly decorated our bedroom, the one I had waited so long for him to finish. He had done such a beautiful job! Life seemed normal again. We had found a church where he felt at home.

In July of that year, my mother visited, and he told her that we were doing well and everything would be just fine. But only a few months later, on that November evening, he chose to walk away from us. And for six long months, I waited every day at 6 p.m., hoping my husband would return home. Every day, I set the table for the three of us. I cooked for three. I truly believed he would come back. I had full faith that God would restore our marriage.

I prayed, fasted, and trusted God. I told him to bring his laundry for me to wash, and I did it with love. I continued to carry myself as his wife and waited for him daily. I believed that one day, after work, he would come home again. I called him and told him he could come whenever he was ready. When he came by to pick up our daughter, drop her off, or take her out, I always treated him as I always had, like my husband. But nothing changed. No matter how much I prayed, pleaded, or asked. He never came back home to us.

Once, I asked him why he didn't want to be with me anymore. His response was that he loved me like a sister, not like a wife. I had to process that answer. I would've preferred if he had told me I was a bad wife. I would've even understood if he had said he loved someone else or that he had slept with another woman. That might have made sense or even justified why he left. But... to love me like a sister?

Very quickly - at least to me - he began the process for our divorce. I refused several times at first. But eventually, I realized that if I didn't agree, a judge could still end the marriage without my consent.

I kept going to the church we used to attend and saw him there... until he stopped going. I continued working, and pretended nothing had happened. Not only that, but I didn't tell anyone at work.

At church, many already knew. I spoke only to those closest to us. From being a married woman in a God-fearing family, I became a divorced woman, a single mother, juggling work, studying, and recovering from a burnout caused by Pfeiffer's disease. To make it worse, my family lived far away, and I didn't receive the support I needed from my church community. It seemed like they weren't prepared to support someone going through something like this.

I shut down. I stopped answering calls. Stopped going to church. I told work I was unwell and entered a medical leave process. I felt rejected and abandoned. I had no strength left, except to return to the survival mode of my youth. I stopped eating, stopped sleeping, and pushed myself just to finish both degree programs. I stopped living. I simply... survived.

I felt like a failure. Like I was worthless. And I also felt like God just sat there and watched. I felt alone and lost.

I had lost everything that gave my life meaning. I lived hour by hour, day by day, convincing myself everything would get better. But things didn't get better. They got worse.

He took off his wedding ring, and I realized there was truly no more hope. I finished both of my degrees carrying the weight of heartbreak. When he hired a lawyer to initiate the divorce, I found myself sitting across from someone I no longer recognized. To me, he was a traitor.

A betrayal by the man I loved, the man I had waited for. A betrayal by his family who had known long before I did that their son would leave his family. A betrayal by the brothers and sisters in Christ who, I felt, had made little effort to support me. I even felt betrayed by God. In my eyes, I had believed and trusted Him with everything in me and yet, He didn't intervene when I needed Him most.

My whole world fell apart. What I feared the most - what I had once judged in others - had now happened to me. I became a single mother. Alone with my daughter. Not knowing what it truly meant to be on my own.

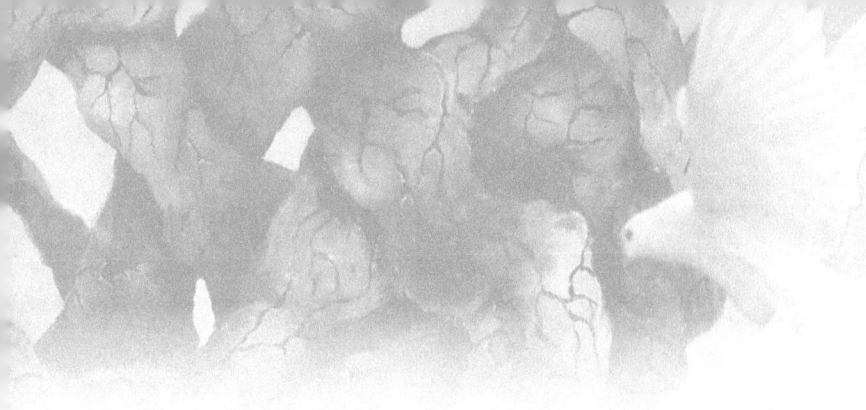

DEPTH

If I remain floating on the surface,
All I'll see is water.
Big waves might cover me,
And even drown me.
But if I dive deep,
And explore the depths of the blue sea,
I'll find a paradise
That I would never see from the surface.

Dive into the Word of the Lord,
Study it daily with passion,
Meditate and memorize until it becomes
part of you.
You will discover the treasure of God
That He has prepared in love for us.

And when the waves of trials rise,
Surely you will overcome
Because just like the sea's waters
surround you,
The Word of God will also carry you.

Let the waves rise
As high as they may
I am not afraid of them.
For I have read it in His Word:
God holds me in His hand,
And nothing and no one can take me
away from Him.

8. AMPUTATION

*"Divorce is like an amputation; you survive,
but there's less of you."*

~ *Margaret Atwood* ~

About a year after my daughter's father left, I traveled to Curaçao for vacation and applied for work. That same month, the divorce papers arrived for me to sign, and I did. That same month, I got a job in Curaçao. Six months later, my daughter and I moved back. And just like that, I was back in my mother's house. She had been right all along.

I lost my husband... I lost my best friend. Until then, I had never really known what it meant to be alone. I went from my parents' house to living with a Dutch family, then into my own place, only to soon share it with the man who would become my husband. I became a mother early in life, and somewhere along the way, I skipped the part where I got to grow into myself. I never truly gave myself the space to discover who I was as a young woman.

I became a mother before I had formed a strong identity of my own, who I was and what I truly wanted. After living together with a friend and then with another family, we eventually built our own life. But I was never truly alone, nor had I learned to do anything independently. I had lived a structured and organized life. In the church I served, I was taught to be a woman for my husband and a servant in my home. My life had meaning and purpose: with a man, I felt like a woman;

with a child, I felt like a mother; and serving in God's house, I felt useful.

Living for God gave me a reason to exist. But now that all of that had fallen apart, now that he was no longer there, what was left? I didn't marry to get divorced! I felt ashamed and guilty. I absorbed those feelings deeply and focused on the one thing my daughter and I needed to survive...

Work. Work and more work. Like a robot, I would take care of my daughter, drop her off at school, and go to work. My life had lost its meaning. I had no strength left for myself, just barely enough for my daughter. The things I once lived for, I could no longer carry. My husband and my daughter had been the center of my existence. With them, I knew how to walk, how to move through this world.

"How can a man of God leave his wife and his child?" my daughter once asked me. I had no answer.

So many questions remained unanswered. I couldn't cope with not having those answers. Throughout my life, I had seen many relationships fall apart and couples divorce or separated; including my own parents. I knew it was something that could happen. But not to me! Not me, who loved God and served Him. Not me, if I was a good woman who had done - the way I experienced it - everything within her power to work on our marriage. Not me...

But then the question returned; why them and not me? It was arrogant and naïve of me to judge others and think it would never come to my doorstep.

We both failed. We both walked away. We both drifted, filling our lives with other things. We both neglected each other and our relationship. Religiousness had become our foundation.

Lying in bed, I felt like a part of me had been removed. Like something essential had been cut away from my body and it hurt deeply. It was as if someone had amputated my leg.

Thinking about it deeply, what I knew was that an amputation is when a doctor has to surgically remove a body part for various reasons. After an accident, injury, disease, burn, or tumor. Some babies are born with a part already missing. I remember reading that when amputation is not an emergency, patients are given time to prepare mentally and physically for what's about to happen. This preparation helps the surgery and recovery go better. After the surgery, patients receive treatment to prevent pain and complications. Rehabilitation is crucial to help them emotionally and physically adjust to life without the missing part.

Amputation can also happen when someone is born with a severely deformed limb due to a genetic condition. It may also be necessary in cases of bone tumors or infections. In situations like an explosion injury, a surgeon may have to remove a foot or an arm. Diabetes can also lead to amputations, especially when circulation is poor and tissue starts to die. Once that tissue is beyond repair, it has to be removed.

I read more about the process and found that before surgery, doctors do a full examination of the area to be amputated. In emergencies, that process is sped up. Physical and psychological tests are also done. Patients are guided through what to expect in their home, work, school, and social life. They may speak with physiotherapists and prosthetic specialists. They may even talk to others who've gone through the same thing. Good preparation and adequate information help recovery.

I became increasingly drawn to the subject. I began to reflect deeply on myself. I felt like a part of me had been cut off. Amputated. I kept researching and learned that the operation is done under anesthesia, meaning the patient is completely unconscious.

Depending on the level of amputation, the doctors may numb half the body or just the affected part. The surgeon separates the body part and uses techniques to restore function in what remains. The goal is to minimize complications. Afterward, the wound is stitched or stapled, and a drainage system is placed. Patients receive oxygen and pain medication.

What follows is vital! Guidance. Pain relief for the physical pain. Psychological help for emotional pain. Rehabilitation through physical therapy.

They explained that phantom pain and sensations often happen after this kind of operation. It's complex. Phantom sensations are when a person feels like the missing limb is still there. Phantom pain is when someone experiences pain in a limb that's no longer present. The pain can be constant or sudden like an attack. It can feel like burning, stabbing, pulling, or cramping.

The reason lies in the brain. The brain still registers that missing part. Now that the body part is gone, the area in the brain that used to connect to it becomes inactive. That disconnection causes the brain to become hypersensitive, registering all stimuli as pain in the amputated area.

I kept staring ahead, as the world around me blurred. I realized that even the memory of pain can manifest as phantom pain. Often, it's the emotional pain a person felt before or during the amputation. The literature I read called it psychological phantom pain.

That is the kind of pain a person associates with a place, an event, a feeling, a person or even a sound. Even though the person is recovering, complications can still emerge physically and psychologically. The sound of the phone ringing pulled me out of my moment of reading and reflection, but I didn't answer it. What I had just read impacted me more deeply than I could have imagined.

I experienced divorce from my marriage and separation from the church like an amputation! And now the process of living without a part of my body had to begin. Every day, I still felt like a married person yet I was not. Anxiety became part of my life. I started rebelling. I went online, looking for a new partner. I spent my days behind the computer, chatting with different men. I was looking for attention, affection, and love from strangers. I had no experience and didn't know how to deal with these fleeting emotions.

I abandoned my friendships, I abandoned the church, and I abandoned God. I thought a group of people who called themselves Christians could not help me. The word hypocrites came out of my mouth almost unconsciously.

I had given - or better said, sacrificed - my life and marriage for the church, and what I got in return was a lack of awareness in this area. Who told me to?

I had placed too much importance on them. Let them stay over there with their judgment. I was going to take another path. And so I did. I poured out my frustration and disappointment through smoking, eating, drinking, going out, and yes; even sleeping around.

I started going to clubs where I sang out loud while dancing out my anger. This time, it wasn't worship or tears that felt like oil on the tips of my fingers. No, this time it was rage. A worshipper, someone who used to minister and guide, now lost in her own wound. It felt like everything had been a lie. Makeup and stylish clothes were covering my wounds, my pain, and my loneliness, all while I was losing my dignity.

With my hands in the air to the beat of trance and house music, only to wake up the next morning and live with the fact that I had quenched my thirst, my loneliness, and my hunger for love with a man I didn't even know. I had suffered an amputation, and complications had occurred. Physically and psychologically.

With everything inside of me, I was resisting this reality. I didn't want to let go or accept this new life. That became the root of the depression I fell into for the following years.

I'M DONE.
I CAN'T KEEP DOING THIS

Why keep denying, why stay angry?
Why keep fighting, why keep struggling?
Did they help me find a solution? Huh?
NO! Only more disappointment.
A deep sadness took root in my heart,
and its tree bore a bitter fruit called...
depression.
I didn't want to deal with anyone or any
situation.
I raised a tall wall around me on all sides...
Isolation!
Don't comfort me, don't encourage me.
Don't talk to me, don't say anything. All
words feel empty
bells that ring, and their sound... just

disappears.

Now the light has gone out, and darkness surrounds me on all sides.

Pain and suffering rule my life. I've entered a dead-end street.

It's enough. I'm throwing in the towel...

As my soul touches the ground, somewhere far away, I hear the sound of celebration.

Is it my enemies rejoicing now that I've been defeated?

Desperate, I struggle and manage to raise a hand.

Is there a door with someone willing to help me up from here?

Because even though depression has taken control of my heart, there's still a small light burning, giving me the hope that maybe... maybe I can still make it.

Please... give me your hand!

9. DEPRESSION

I always heard people say you can't run from your problems or situations. One year, one day... they will catch up to you.

When I packed my bags and sent them ahead to Curaçao, I took all my personal baggage with me, baggage I had never really dealt with. I put make-up on my face and dressed well on the outside, but my soul, with all its emotional wounds, traveled with me. All my insecurities, pain, and anxieties came too.

In my arms, my daughter - my only child - carried her own baggage. Not only the literal bags but also emotional ones. We say "one plus one equals two," but for me, back then, one plus one felt incalculable. Fears of inadequacy, rejection, and self-doubt became a fortress around me, though I refused to fully accept it.

Disconnected from faith and hope, I returned to Curaçao, to start anew.

In January 2006, I returned with my daughter and moved in with my parents. The house we had in the Netherlands was up for sale, and I chose not to bring anything from it except our clothes and my daughter's toys and things that were important to her: her books, and also emotional items like pictures and my books.

Back in my parents' house. My father no longer lived there, it was my mother and my brother now. My daughter got her own room, and I moved into the apartment space downstairs. It didn't take long before I wanted to leave again. I eventually moved more than ten times. For us, packing and moving became a lifestyle. Instability became synonymous with my life.

I became someone else. I worked a lot. My daughter often stayed with her grandmother while I processed my grief. I kept my eyes on what had happened to me and had no energy left to focus on anything else. I stayed busy with work while emotionally withdrawing from people, dwelling inside my own world of feelings.

Because of my passion and focus, I began to grow professionally, as a social worker and personal development trainer. I gave so much of myself to help, guide, and support others. But after a long workday, I had no energy left, except to fall back into sadness, disappointment, guilt, and anger. I made myself a victim, and unconsciously I chose to stay there.

About a year and a half after I arrived in Curaçao, I met a man. I had promised myself I would never again date a Christian man or a so-called "man of God." Because if these things happen inside the church, then I'd rather look outside of it. At least there, I would know what I was getting into. That was one of the biggest lies I lived through, because in truth, I had no idea what I was getting into.

Remember, I was a wife, a faithful and loyal woman, someone who took care of her family and put them first. A woman who knew what it meant to submit, to serve, and to love. A dedicated woman who had tasted mercy, grace, and the love of God. A woman who believed in holiness even when I struggled to keep my own sanity. A woman who prayed about everything and reflected deeply before making decisions.

I didn't realize the weight of my words.

Because I ended up with a man, older and more experienced in life and the streets. He was a teacher. A man constantly battling his own darkness. He had two sides, gentle and caring on one hand, but he easily became a heavy drinker and marijuana user on the other. He had other women I didn't know about at the time. He would disappear for days in very strange ways.

Then he'd return, sleep with me, and sleep for 24 hours straight. There was something rugged about him that I found strangely attractive. Like he felt free. That's why I couldn't get a grip on him. Every time he left and came back, there was so much manipulation and sweet talk that I accepted all his recklessness. Did I not deserve better? I had asked for this, yet I couldn't handle it. What did I know about men like him? Nothing!

Protected for so long behind the walls of the church, I had no idea how to handle this. I experienced things I'd only heard about, things I'd seen in movies.

I loved reading, but I had never bought or read books on subjects like this. Too heavy. Too unfamiliar.

There was cheating, emotional abuse, and intense drug and alcohol use. I had to deal with a body marked by other women, with manipulation, fear, and anxiety. All this while raising a child. But no! Being a single mom wasn't enough. I had to also prove I was still a "woman." No matter the cost.

That situation contributed to the final crack in my being. I lost everything, because I lost myself. And that, I called "love." Another lie!

The relationship ended at the end of 2007. The situation escalated to the point where I had a panic attack combined with hysteria. After a heated argument, I got into my car and drove off. At first, I was just driving but then my breathing got tight. My heart was out of control, beating like an airplane engine. My vision started going dark.

I began trembling and hyperventilating, gripped by a sudden wave of fear. I screamed and cried hysterically. I felt like either I had to drive my car as fast as I could or get out and run with no destination. Everything felt like it was crashing down on me. I broke out in sweats, hot and cold at the same time. I pulled over and called a colleague who had become a friend.

She understood me. She accepted me without judgment. No one else knew how deeply I was struggling emotionally. At work, I was performing excellently. No one suspected how badly I was doing inside.

She dropped everything and came to get me. She brought me to the doctor. There, I was given a tranquilizer that knocked me out for twelve hours. Afterward, she brought me home, and I went to sleep.

That peace didn't last more than six hours. Soon I felt like I was losing my mind again.

A few days later, I saw a psychologist. Shortly after that, I was hospitalized with depression, insomnia, and panic attacks. It was the moment of the "perfect storm." Everything came crashing together at once creating a total catastrophe. There was nothing anyone could do. Nothing anyone could do for me, except sedate me and give me medications to regulate my emotions.

Before and after my hospitalization, my life focus was work. Again.. That's all that took up my energy. I couldn't deal with bad news, disappointment, conflict, or anything that disturbed my peace. I lived either in the past, blaming myself, or worrying about a future that felt insecure. I feared everything.

Fear of being hurt again. Fear of being used. Fear of being judged. Fear of dying because I didn't want my daughter to suffer. But also, the desire to die because I didn't want to face life.

Life felt like too much. I couldn't handle it.

I didn't feel at home in the world I was living in. I didn't feel like I belonged or even should be here. I longed for peace. For happiness. For another reality. But I searched for all of that outside of myself.

At work, my daughter, in friends and in helping others. But nowhere could I find what I was truly looking for.

On the contrary, how I saw myself became smaller with every passing day. And for reasons that were my own doing. I kept expecting people around me to make me happy, something no one else could ever do.

Little by little, I withdrew even more into isolation where my negative thoughts took over.

Everything began and ended with thoughts of criticism, self-contempt, and hopelessness. I felt like I was literally losing myself in darkness and didn't know how to get out. Everything I did or didn't do had its root in fear and desperation. I wanted my old life back. I wanted to be married again, a stable mother, a woman of faith and who longed for safety.

I didn't want to accept that I was no longer there. I wanted to, but I didn't know how. How to build a new life? I didn't know how to give meaning to my existence again. I blamed myself completely for not being able to save my marriage. A social worker! Me! How could I see so much, understand where so many things came from, know people, work with people, help people...

Yet I couldn't save my own marriage. I couldn't even help myself so I could be strong for my one and only daughter. Very quickly, the realization that I couldn't even be there for my child took over. It became a constant whisper: Now, I wasn't just a wife who had failed, I was a mother who had failed. And in my own eyes, that made me a woman who had failed entirely. My self-worth sank to the bottom. I stopped living and started merely existing.

The nights were especially hard. I couldn't sleep. My pillows were soaked with tears. Sleeping pills helped me doze off. I felt tired, but I couldn't fall asleep. My mind kept racing. When I opened my eyes in the morning, I immediately started crying. I had no strength to get up, wash myself, and go to work again. I'd almost fall back into the same cycle.

I neglected everything; myself, my daughter, and my home. For a few years, I lived in constant "ups and downs" super happy days that felt manic, followed by crashing back into a depression I couldn't climb out of.

That's how I lived, day in and day out. The only thing that kept going well - thanks to God - was my work. Because of the deep passion I had for what I did, it was the one stable thing in my life. So I sought refuge in my work, in my career, and I kept growing as a professional.

There were moments when I'd be driving and suddenly have a panic attack. I'd cry and scream, then park my car somewhere isolated to take medication or just try to calm down. Other times, I would completely dissociate. But thank God, someone always seemed to show up right on time. People from the neighborhood who somehow intervened before anything tragic happened.

Nothing could make me happy for more than a moment. I felt so low that whatever I tried to add to my life just seemed to leak out the other side. I went to a psychologist, psychiatrist, pastors, spoke to friends, sought advice and support from my sibling, and looked for love in a man. In my desperation, I even visited churches, but I always walked away realizing it wasn't just the divorce they didn't understand. They couldn't understand the depression either.

Nothing helped. I was tired... tired of myself, tired of everything. My panic attacks would sometimes result in speeding while driving, hitting myself in the face or body, crying and screaming hysterically or otherwise, just sleeping. Sleeping, hoping I wouldn't wake up again. When I wasn't feeling that extreme, I tried to live my life as normally as possible.

What makes depression so hard is that it creeps in quietly. You don't know exactly when it begins. By the time I realized I was depressed, I had already been living in it for three years. It started subtly, like a slow leak in my mind. At first, just a faint drip... drip barely noticeable. Then silence. You think it's stopped. But beneath the surface, the water keeps rising. Until one day, it spills over and floods everything. That's what happened to me.

By the time I started experiencing the physical symptoms that came with it, it was too late. When I started to feel sick, when I finally realized something wasn't right, I was already deep in the illness. But I had no idea. How was I supposed to get out of this dark world?

How could I talk to someone about it, knowing I'd be labeled for life?

They couldn't see me going to a psychologist or psychiatrist, because only "crazy" people go there, right? Loneliness had taken over. I felt completely alone. And nobody understood me. Not even I understood myself. I felt like a stranger. Was I crazy? Was I unstable or had I lost my mind?

That's how I felt, because I couldn't function as a mother and couldn't live in a healthy and stable relationship. Why couldn't I get out of this? I had no value. I didn't belong anywhere. The fact that I couldn't "succeed" only confirmed again and again: I wasn't enough. And the voice kept echoing: "See? You really are worthless!"

I wanted to be here for my daughter and yet, at the same time, I didn't want to be part of this world anymore. I longed for a different life. There were moments when I asked God to take me. I wanted to live for my daughter, but I didn't feel I had the strength. I wanted an easy way out. I prayed to fall asleep and not wake up again, yet every morning I still thanked God that I did wake up for my daughter's sake. My life no longer had meaning, and I felt utterly alone. Completely abandoned.

I asked myself: How does someone climb out of a pit this deep? How do you restore your self-image, confidence, and self-worth when there's almost nothing left?

I would get out of those thoughts momentarily, but then return to the same cycle worse than before. Because now my decisions were based on how low I thought of myself. The results and consequences only confirmed my belief: I really wasn't good enough.

I kept choosing men who had no place in my life, disrespectful, distant, and damaging.

Men who cheated on me, who slept with other women. Men who were emotionally unavailable and I kept falling into desperation, where the fear of abandonment controlled me. Maybe that's what I deserved?

After my marriage ended, I started asking myself: What was going on in my head that I accepted a situation that wasn't good for me - or for my daughter - yet I stayed in it? I lowered all my principles, values, morals, and standards.

For what? For what I used to call love? I mixed everything up. Confusion completely took over my life. I no longer knew what self-love was, or self-worth. I didn't even know who I was anymore. I didn't have the strength to put a stop to this vicious cycle.

As my social circle shrank smaller and smaller, I stopped existing. I withdrew from everyone. People would call, but I wouldn't answer. I'd make appointments and cancel them. I stopped doing the things I loved and created a life that felt lifeless.

Four years of high peaks and deep lows... Seasons of better and worse, where I didn't even realize I was passing through depression. I was so exhausted that I didn't even realize there were enough people around me who truly loved me. The support of those who stayed, and the structure of caring for my daughter and home, helped. Combined with my total focus on work, little by little, the moments when I felt somewhat normal and useful began to return, slowly but surely.

It had already been some years since I had decided I wouldn't take any more medication to calm or "fix" anything. That November, I reached a crossroad in my life. By nature, I'm a very sensitive person who experiences everything intensely. Not just pain, but also the good things, the things I could enjoy and that helped me feel alive.

The medication had turned me into someone numb, like a person who felt nothing anymore. On one hand, it calmed me, but on the other hand, it paralyzed me. It was such a contrast to the energetic person I once was.

In my line of work, I needed to remain empathetic and sensitive to the signals people give. I chose not to live my life that way anymore, so I stopped all medication. First, with the help of my psychiatrist and psychologist, I reduced the dosage. Then I stopped completely, along with all the side effects that came with it. That too was its own process. Not an easy one, but I was so tired, I didn't want it anymore.

I stopped going to therapy and prayed to God daily, asking Him to help me, to heal me from my illness and from all the thoughts and feelings that tormented me.

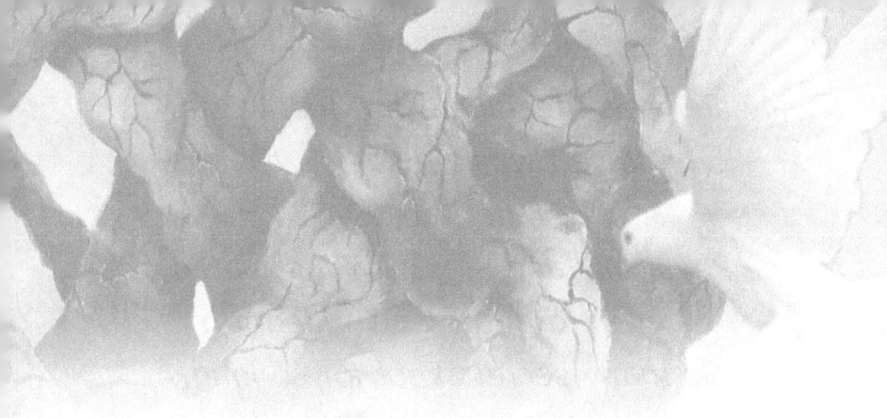

MY INHERITANCE

A mansion, a car, money...my inheritance!
Dazzling jewels,
Crafted from pearls, gold, and diamonds,
my inheritance!
The ability to study and become an
important woman, my inheritance!
It comes from my father, mother,
and also my grandmother.
Even a great-aunt died and left something
behind. That's my inheritance!
No matter how hard I've tried,
I've never managed to succeed.
Financial struggles seem to live at my
doorstep. Is poverty my inheritance?
Sickness clings to me, one after another.

My life feels meaningless. I feel worthless.
Ever since I was abused! Is that my
inheritance?
Physically and mentally mistreated,
I even forgot my own identity.
So many secrets kept for so long..
How do I break the silence?
Lord, my God! ...Is this my inheritance?

No, My child, NO!
For so long, I've waited
For you to pour out your heart before Me
like water.
This moment, I created just for you.
Stop, be still, and realize
That yes, you are My child,
And that makes you My heir.

To you I've given
Three powerful weapons through which,
Today, your chains will be broken:
The Name of Jesus, the Blood of Jesus,
and the Word of Truth.
Rise up, fight, and be set free!

Break every chain of the cursed
inheritance that binds you.

Your inheritance is:
Happiness, not misery.
Real joy that flows without rage.
Those who trust in Me will inherit the land.
I will give you peace, honor,
and wealth now,
And finally, the heavenly inheritance
Eternal life, which your Savior has
prepared in His great love.
*Yes, My child, **this** is your inheritance!*

10. AN OPEN WOUND

While watching a movie, I heard the line: "The wound of honor is self-inflicted."

That means wounds to our honor are often caused by our own actions.

My mind went to the story of the eagle. It can live up to seventy years. But to achieve that, it must make a painful decision. Around forty years old, its claws become too long and curved to catch prey effectively, making it difficult to feed itself.

Its beak, once sharp and strong, begins to bend. Its feathers grow thick and heavy, sticking to its chest and weighing it down. At that point, the eagle has only two choices: die or undergo a painful process of renewal. The eagle must fly to the top of a mountain and sit alone in its nest. There, it beats its beak against a rock until it breaks off. Then, it waits for a new beak to grow.

With that new beak, it plucks out its claws. And once those regrow, it removes the heavy feathers. Only then can it fly again, renewed for another thirty years. A necessary transformation for survival and life.

It was the night of August 10, 2011, when my mother's call came through. She said my brother had gotten sick. She wasn't sure where it happened or what exactly was wrong. All she knew was that he had been taken to the emergency room. Her voice was steady, almost too steady, but I could hear the worry underneath.

My body went cold from the rush of anxiety flooding over me. I called my father and then my sister-in-law to update them. Each of us rushed from where we were to meet at the hospital. Sitting in the waiting room, they called for our family. I walked quickly behind the nurse. Around me, people were moving back and forth. Some were sleeping or waiting. A doctor approached me. I had to lift my head to look into his face as he explained that they couldn't say exactly what was happening yet. "We're still running tests," he told me.

He explained that my brother had collapsed in a nightclub vomiting and foaming at the mouth. An ambulance had been called. As I followed the doctor through the corridor, the sound of screaming grew louder. Then we stopped. The doctor stood still beside a bed with my brother lying there, screaming with his eyes tightly shut.

He was wearing jeans. Shirtless and twisted on the bed. I stared at him with so many questions in my mind while trying to keep myself under control. The nurse who had brought me in handed me his wallet, car keys, phone, watch, and jewelry and told me we'd know more in the morning. The next day, they told us he had suffered a cerebral hemorrhage - a stroke - and was in critical condition in the Intensive Care Unit.

The specialist explained that the next 72 hours would be crucial; it could go either way, recovery or death. We visited him every day and prayed to God for his healing. After three days, he began to improve. They decided to keep him two more days in intensive care before moving him to the men's ward.

I visited him and cared for him every day. I noticed he wasn't fully well yet, speaking in scattered, confused phrases. Still, he seemed to be recovering, talking, eating, even joking at times. On Friday, the specialist called for a meeting. They explained Bryan's condition and said that if he kept improving, he could go home on

Monday. We would need to arrange home care and a wheelchair, as he still couldn't walk properly. He was weak and had lost a lot of weight. We left that meeting filled with hope and gratitude. The next day, Saturday, I returned to see him again.

He looked much better. I felt relieved and lighter. The stress started to lift. I could breathe again. Because I had been going through those intense days while also working, I decided that Sunday I wouldn't go to the hospital. I needed one day off. Now, finally, the rest of the family could visit him too, as he was allowed visitors. So I didn't go.

Sunday night, shortly after 9 PM, after the last visitor had left, the hospital called me. My brother had taken a turn for the worse, and we were asked to come as soon as possible...

Before my father met my mother, he already had two sons and two daughters. They were my half-siblings from his side. My father married my mother, and in

March 1972, my mother had my brother, their firstborn and in November 1973, she had me.

My mother always said that Bryan was planned, but I came as a "surprise". From the beginning, she told us, we were different in almost every way. Bryan was calm, gentle by nature, a little reserved, an introvert who noticed everything. I, on the other hand, was expressive and outgoing, drawn to family and connection, always making sure my presence was known. Even as children, our contrasts were clear. My brother would quietly watch me as I chatted with strangers or refused to sit still, then turn to my mother and ask her to make me stop or to tell me to come sit down.

As we grew older, our differences only became stronger. We could be together and tolerate each other for a while, but very quickly we would each go our separate ways. We would go out together and enjoy ourselves with cousins, mutual friends, and neighborhood kids, but still, each of us stayed in our own lane.

My brother and I were not like siblings who were also best friends. Those who are always together, who talk and share everything, who understand each other deeply. I experienced our relationship more like fire and water, night and day, east and west. We were opposites in every way, and that meant that even though we spent a lot of time in each other's presence, I never felt a deep connection with him. It was more like I felt closer to the flamboyant tree in our yard. The tree our grandmother had planted for my brother. That big, beautiful tree with its seasonal flowers, whose branches I used to climb with my friend.

Whenever I felt close to my brother, it was from a distance. Watching him but never truly connecting. That distance defined our relationship from the start. We argued regularly, and those arguments were intense. The fact that I lived abroad had its advantages. Those were times when we appreciated each other more.

We loved each other deeply, but in a very special and unique way. Sometimes his actions made me feel unappreciated, and I believe he felt the same way about me. I never asked him about it. Still, he was the one I chose to be the godfather of my only child.

As I got older, I emotionally distanced myself even more. Back then, I judged him a lot. I didn't agree with some of the choices he made or how he saw life. There were times I didn't like what he stood for in my eyes. Our differences only grew with time. I knew he loved me because he was always ready to defend me, no matter what.

I remember once I was on vacation in Curaçao and had rented a car. The next day, when I woke up, the car was gone. When my mother told him, he left the house to ask around in the neighborhood to see if anyone had seen anything. I remember him coming back with the news that he knew who did it. Bryan grabbed a baseball bat and was ready to leave the house and handle the situation. Shirtless and furious, he stormed down the stairs and shouted that no one messes with his sister. It was only my and my mother's pleading that stopped him from going out and doing something drastic.

Moments like that, those kinds of situations, he showed up for me. In those moments, I felt like the little sister being protected by her big brother. I spent years longing for a better relationship with my brother. But I didn't know how to make that happen. Because I didn't know better, I never gave him a fair chance to show me who he really was. I didn't want to accept who he was or the life he had chosen for himself. I was waiting for him to change first. Why I waited, I don't know. But in doing so, I robbed myself of the chance to have a better bond with him.

I judged him. I remember once he told me that a man could sleep with another woman and still love his partner. Well... that made me even more angry with him. How could he think like that? How could my brother believe such a thing? I was naïve and inexperienced. I strongly disagreed with how he handled his relationships, and I wanted nothing to do with those parts of his life. I rejected the things he said and did. In doing so, I was rejecting him as a person. I even went as far as moving out of the house I shared with him and our mother because we didn't get along.

Years later, on the night of December 31, 2009, Bryan was in a serious car accident. He crashed into someone's front yard and completely destroyed a wall. His car was completely wrecked. That night, he escaped death for the second time. As a young man, he once drove my mother's brand-new Ford Thunderbird bought in Miami and crashed it too. That car was completely destroyed as well. He had escaped death by a hair's breadth.

But not this time!

This time, when the hospital called us to come as quickly as possible, I drove over and parked. As I stepped out of the car, I heard someone screaming; loudly! As I approached the hospital entrance, I recognized the voice. It was my brother. He was screaming nonstop. Climbing the stairs to his room, my heart pounded in my chest.

Adrenaline rushed through my veins, and I lost all sense of what was happening around me. My feet moved faster than my body. What was going on? Why was he screaming like that? My God, help us! I didn't know what to do. Fear gripped me. Fear and helplessness. I stood frozen at the door of the room.

What I saw never left me. It clings to my sight, lingers in my thoughts. Marked. Even now. To this day. My brother was tied up. Restraint straps held his arms and legs in place on the bed. Yet he was twisting and shaking, trying to break free. His screaming now turned into agony. He ripped himself loose, struggling with uncontrollable force. His eyes were wide open, but it was like he couldn't see. He didn't see me...

I was in shock! I felt myself falling backward, again and again, until the nurse yelled for my help.

"Help me!" she screamed.

I stood a little farther away, repeatedly asking her, "What happened? What happened?"

The nurse on duty explained that Bryan had been fine, talking earlier with her, but suddenly he started behaving this way. They were understaffed at the time, so she asked for my help to restrain him.

At that moment, I went into autopilot. I began moving on instinct, disconnected from all emotions. This life-or-death situation flipped a switch, and I helped the nurse hold Bryan down and restrain him again properly on the bed. Meanwhile, the mother of his daughter -

his partner - arrived.

Together; his partner, the nurse, and I rushed through the hospital halls with Bryan on the bed to get him to the MRI room. It was critical for him to remain still during the scan. As we stood there, his partner tried to calm him and keep him still, but by then, we could no longer reach him. His eyes were closed tight, but he was still moving, shaking and peeing himself... Though we were all there, we could do nothing.

My ears caught the nurse's conversation on the phone with the doctor. She explained this was a first-time experience for her, and she noted they had given Bryan a lot of sedatives to calm him, but it wasn't working. We remained there, holding him... I don't know for how long... until he finally calmed down enough to place him in the machine.

We left the MRI room and returned to the waiting area where we found my parents. I explained to them once again what had happened.

Waiting! It's something that, for many people, is difficult. But for me, it was a nightmare.

I experienced the act of waiting as something deeply distressing. Waiting left me in a state of uncertainty mixed with powerlessness. I didn't know what was going to happen... I didn't know what to expect. And I had no control.

And in this case, nothing was in my hands.

I could do nothing. And while I waited, time itself became the greatest challenge for me, because what I did - or didn't do - during that waiting period felt incredibly insignificant.

They isolated my brother. Meanwhile, my niece had arrived. I had called my sister, Judy, to come, but her husband told us she was sleeping.

Me, my mother, my father, my brother's partner, and my niece were all together with Bryan in his hospital room. Waiting... the minutes passed slowly. No one could tell us what had happened to Bryan. They had taken images of his brain, but the neurologist on call had not yet arrived. After we insisted on seeing the doctor, the nurse told us they had called him repeatedly, but he still hadn't shown up.

We were all gathered in my brother's room. Except for my mom. She told me she didn't want to see her son like that. The nurse encouraged me to bring my mom to Bryan. I tried again, but she remained standing off to the side, choosing instead to sit alone and pray, believing God would intervene.

Finally, the doctor arrived. The smell of alcohol clung to him. He spoke to me, and his smell was overwhelming. My stomach twisted and nausea gripped me. I felt like vomiting everything inside me. He told me Bryan had suffered a second brain hemorrhages, and that nothing else could be done. Just like that, he told me in Dutch:

"It's his own fault. That's how they destroy their bodies."

I imagined myself throwing up all the hostility and shame that had built up inside me, projecting it onto him, letting it splatter across his smug face. I imagined it dripping off his skin.

"You were at De Heeren, weren't you?

That late hour, when the restaurant dims and turns into a bar

I overheard the nurse, when she called you over and over again.

You were drinking.

Drinking, when you were the specialist who was supposed to be here. And now you're standing in front of me, telling me this reeking of alcohol?"

I wanted to scream, to ask him who he thought he was. What right he had to break every code of ethics and professionalism and insult both me and my defenseless brother. At that moment, I wanted to grab a bat and hit him. But I said nothing. Not one word. I turned and walked away...

I went to find my mother again. And once more, she told me she didn't want to enter the room.

I returned to Bryan's room. From a distance, I saw him sleeping. He was breathing strangely. I could hear the mucus in his breath. He lay on his right side. His eyes had remained shut since the scan. My niece was talking to him and reading Bible verses. His partner stood on the other side, stroking his head. My father stood next to me, with folded hands.

Without realizing it, I walked over to Bryan. I kissed him gently and whispered in his ear that I loved him, and I asked him to forgive me for everything... Especially for the things I never asked forgiveness for. Things I did knowingly and unknowingly. Things I remembered, and those I had forgotten. The things I regretted and the ones I hadn't found the courage to regret yet.

Not long after that, the sound of the mucus stopped. Moments later, I couldn't hear anything anymore. My niece turned and said she believed Bryan was no longer breathing. We called the nurse. A doctor was summoned. And just like that, at 1:08 a.m., a doctor confirmed his death.

And even then, a tear slid from my brother's closed eyes...

...And with trembling legs, I went to find my mother. The distance between my brother's room and where my mother sat wasn't far, yet it became one of the longest and heaviest walks I've ever taken in my life. She was sitting in the hallway outside his room on the first floor. This time, I didn't ask her to come. I said, "Mama, let's go see Bryan."

She responded, "Why?"

I said, "Mom... he's gone. We just lost him."

I took her gently down the hallway to his room. Everyone was already there, tears streaming down their faces. Making the inevitable visible. Crying!

And my mother... She entered, stood still, and gazed at her son - our Bryan - and in shock, not a single tear escaped her eyes, though I am sure a river of tears flowed inside. A mother sees her son dead and not the other way around. There are no words. You break. Life changes instantly. We stayed there until the funeral home staff came to collect him.

He passed away on August 22, 2011. The double brain hemorrhage had taken his life. The next morning, August 23, my mother cried in the company of Judy. On August 27, 2011, we laid him to rest.

Remarkably, as we sat together sharing stories after the burial, I heard one of his closest friends recount something peculiar. Bryan had told him, about six months earlier, that he felt like an eagle ready for transformation. At the time of that statement, Bryan had just turned thirty-nine. He left us less than six months later. God took him.

In one way or another, my life changed course after my brother died. Not only because I became the only child from my mother and father's marriage, but also because I was living on my own and then returned to live at home again, because my mother was left alone.

After Bryan passed, we found ourselves dealing with not only his death but also unresolved matters left behind, both material and immaterial.

Imagine this: my mother and brother had lived together all the time I was abroad. A few years before Bryan passed, with the consent of my elders, he bought our family home for a symbolic price to help my parents with what was left of the mortgage. He and my mother had signed the necessary documents. The verbal agreement was that he would buy the house for the remaining mortgage balance left at the bank, but that the house would remain ours - shared among the four of us - and later be sold, with the proceeds distributed equally as inheritance.

Everything had gone through a notary. Neither I nor Judy were part of the process, and I wasn't aware of the exact conditions.

When my brother died, I came to realize that they had never officially registered the verbal agreement between my mom and brother with the notary.

Because who would have expected that he'd die less than two years later? Bryan passed away without formalizing the agreements about the inheritance. Bryan had a daughter, who was seven years old at the time of his death. And automatically, that child became the full heir of what should have been shared among all of us.

Waiting to change, waiting to forgive, waiting to mature, waiting to restore, waiting to accept, waiting to make things right, waiting to fix and handle matters, waiting to recognize, waiting to ask for forgiveness, waiting to live and love?

Why wait until acting is your only option?

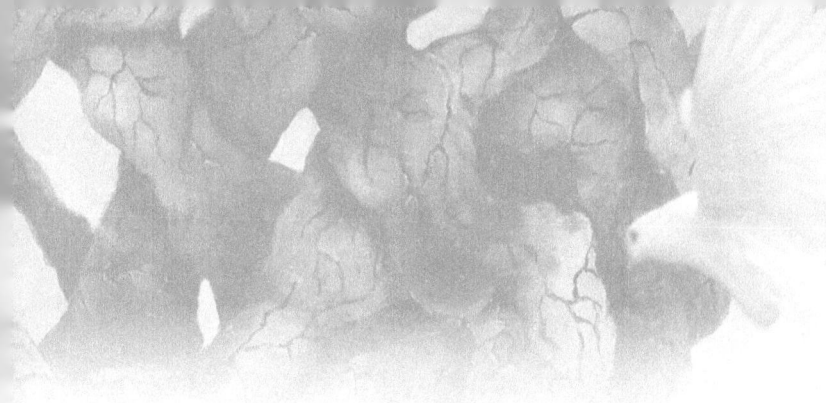

SIGHT OR FAITH?

I have come to realize
That even though sight is of great
importance,
Many times, our eyes cannot capture
The most important things in our lives.
When night falls, I cannot see the sun,
But its influence still preserves nature.
I cannot see the wind,
yet it refreshes my body.
I cannot see oxygen, but without it,
I cannot live.

Still, people want to see first in
order to believe.
No! People choose when they want to

see before they believe.
What suits us, we believe without seeing.
And what does not suit us, we question,
Declaring that only when we see it,
we will believe.

I have realized that this doesn't work.
It costs me too much energy to argue,
Forcing my mind to search for a formula
And yet nothing becomes clear.

I choose to dive into the river of Faith, to
believe what I do not see,
Trusting that what I hope for will surely
come to pass.
This experience has given me peace,
And combined with patience, I have
achieved so much more.

I want to invite you to try it too.
You have nothing to lose,
Because everything is possible for the one
who has Faith.

11. LOAD ON MY BACK

I was tired of living my life feeling dead. In my mind, I knew what to do to get out. That's what I had been telling other people. I was a therapist myself. I knew what to do. I knew what the books and the literature said. I knew what I had learned in my studies and what I had seen work for more than a decade. I had successfully helped so many people help themselves! I heard their testimonies all the time.

How was it possible that I had no idea what to do with myself?

That realization hit me in the face.

I was like someone who spits in the air, only to have the spit fall right back on their own head. I was giving to others what I didn't even have for myself. I couldn't see a positive ending for my own life, making it difficult to see the light in my own tunnel. And yet, everything has its why and its reason; I just needed to see and extract the good I could find in them.

Through my new partner of two years - who was also a great support in my professional development - I learned about a "Dance Therapy Intensive Course" on Long Island, New York. It was a course to become a dance therapist, a therapy that analyzes movement and expresses emotions through dancing to intentionally selected music. It's something that greatly supports healing, especially when words become too difficult to express.

He offered to pay for it, and after hesitating, I went. It had only been three months since I buried my brother, and everything still felt like it had just happened to all of us. It was my first time traveling completely alone and far away. With my ticket already booked and paid for, I couldn't back out. It's strange how sometimes what you need the most is what you least want to do.

In December, I flew to New York. It was my first trip alone to such a big place, during the holiday season, far from everyone and everything. A completely new experience for me—especially since I didn't like or know how to do anything on my own. Those two weeks were the beginning of my healing from what I had been carrying for a large part of my life.

I danced... danced... and danced every day, all day, but now to the music of transformation. Learning the theory and techniques of the therapy. Everything we learned, they had us practice first on ourselves. I danced and expressed all the pain, disappointment, anger, and emotions I hadn't even realized I had.

During one of the sessions, it became clear that I was carrying everything on my back. I even walked and danced bent over... with a weight, a burden on me. And that day, at that moment, I danced and physically laid down all the things I had been carrying. I danced, screamed, cried and afterward, felt relieved and light again. The situation hadn't completely changed, because emotionally I still felt unstable. But I had laid down much of the weight, creating space to deal with all that was still happening and needed to happen.

I returned to Curaçao with my dance therapy certificate and lighter baggage. Little by little, but steadily, I learned to channel my emotions better through dance and singing songs that uplift, or songs of worship. I began to work on myself: recognizing, accepting, and attending to myself. Realizing that the one who needed to change was me.

I read a lot. I went to the beach every Saturday. Alone. I would talk to God. I knew I needed to make the decision to let in everything positive and good for me. I even changed the way I watched television and read the news. I stopped allowing negative things to enter my system and made room for things that would strengthen me more.

In my fight for a better mental and emotional state, finally, in March 2013, five months after I returned to Curaçao from NY something strange and very surreal happened. It was a day like any other, and yet, by the end of that day , as if reality had been unveiled - suddenly - I could see clearly. My mind opened up to a specific area in my way of thinking. What had entangled my life for so long made space for the night to turn into day. Suddenly, I saw life in a way I never had before.

The beginning of a new stage in my life took place.

Many times, people tell you so many things. Somehow you know and even understand what they're telling you. Your mind captures it, but it hasn't yet found its place in your heart or vice versa. An internal struggle happens. You think about it, but you don't believe it yet. You know, but it hasn't yet become reality in your life.

My half-sister, though in truth there was never anything "half" about her, Judy called me once again. She has been a lifeline in my life, loving me unconditionally and asking for nothing in return. Judy has always met me where I was, without judgment, offering love and gentleness, and speaking truth wrapped in compassion and wisdom. She never tried to fix me, only to be with me. Fully, honestly, and always in truth.

So many times she would call me, and I couldn't or didn't want to answer. She didn't condemn me and remained patient.

That night, something was different.

She called, and somehow, I answered. I didn't want to have contact with anyone. She listened to me on the phone. The same old story came out of my mouth. The same negativity. The same narrative, where I would again bring up my pain, disappointment, and feelings of darkness. I played the role of victim and felt sorry for myself for the thousandth time.

After listening to me, she described a story to me.

"When God created birds, initially they didn't have wings. They moved around only using their little legs, and they were happy. God watched them and knew they weren't complete yet. He decided that He would make wings for them. And that's what He did. He made wings for them and placed them on their backs. The birds weren't happy with what God had done for them. They complained and went to God, indicating that the wings weren't nice for them to have. The wings were too heavy. They had no idea what to do with them. They kept complaining to God, saying they were carrying something so uncomfortable, for nothing. God then explained to them that they had wings for a purpose. There was a valid reason why He had created special wings for them. And the reason was so they would be free. They would be able to see all creation from above and travel whenever needed to overcome obstacles that would arise. They would be able to see heaven and earth entirely from another perspective. The wings would make them swift and able to move with the wind. They were the instruments for them to be complete."

Judy continued:

"Sis... you keep seeing everything that has happened in your life as a weight. A heavy burden. You only see what happened to you, but you don't realize that God allowed those things in your life for a reason... a purpose. God placed wings on your back. They may feel heavy, and maybe you don't understand why you have them. Sis, you have wings on your back. Stop seeing them as a burden. Use them to fly. Look now at all you've learned from these situations and use them for good."

And suddenly... very suddenly... The message touched me!

The veil I had over my eyes fell. My vision cleared. Suddenly, I understood. Deep within my soul, I understood and accepted.

The very things I had in my mind and heart that were holding me down were my strength. If I would just change how I saw them, I would understand. And standing there - on a deep level - I realized they were precisely my strength. They had shaped me, and that, in truth, there was a reason and a purpose for everything.

And at that moment... precisely that moment, I was ready to allow the new thought to enter and let go of all the negative feelings and emotions.

I saw my suffering as part of what had shaped me into a woman with experience and compassion. A woman who understands others because she herself has been through it. A woman who extracts the best from every situation and truly forgives. A woman who uses what once pressed her life down to lift others up, with love, patience, and gentleness.

Somehow, I came to recognize - despite everything - how many good things and valuable life lessons those very hardships had taught and brought me. Everything changed in that moment because my way of thinking changed. In the blink of an eye, I found answers to my years-long prayers. I realized that God had heard me and answered me. He gave me what I needed at the moment He knew I was ready to receive it.

A mental shift took place, like a light turning on in the dark. I knew what to do with the burdens - or better said - the wings on my back.

I decided I would use them. I would use them to fly. In this way, all my experiences gained meaning, destiny, and purpose!

I stopped focusing on what I didn't have and fixed my gaze on all that I did have.

I opened my heart, and immediately, understanding, wisdom, and true love began to enter powerfully into my life.

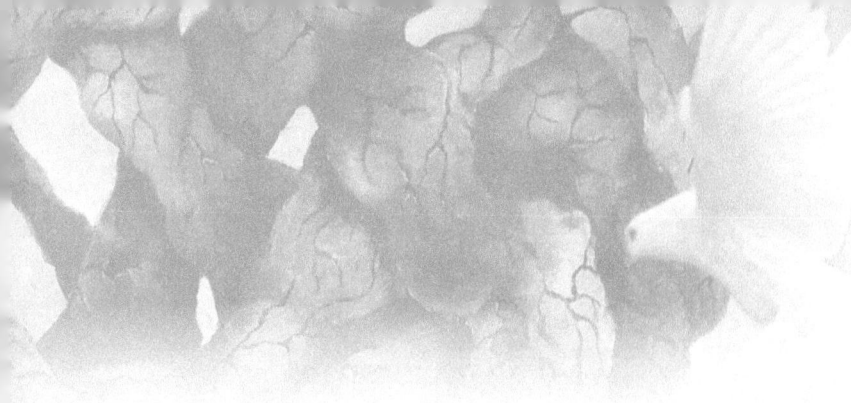

PEACE

What is peace?
Stillness without disturbance?
Sleep without nightmares?
Work without pressure?
A sea without waves?
A waterfall without sound?

So what is peace, then?
Victory without battle?
A journey without turbulence?
A race without competition?
A road without obstacles?
A life without challenges?

No, peace is not tied to circumstances.
No, peace is not about falling or rising.

Peace is the product of trust.
Peace is the fruit of security.
The root of peace is faith.
Peace always remains,
despite the unfavorable circumstances
we may go through.

Now, trust, security, and faith in whom?
In the Prince of Peace,
who left us an example.
He endured pain, suffering, and injustice.
And even though He wrestled with
the grip of death,
still... in the end,
He managed to maintain His peace.

Now, is this possible for humans?
Has that question crossed your mind?
It may be difficult, but... impossible? Never!
The Father promised that He would never
give us a burden too heavy for us to carry.
And the Holy Spirit gives us the grace to
reach it.

He Himself declared:
"My peace I leave with you. My peace I give to you."

PEACE...
People who don't have God will never experience it.
But you - yes, you - and I who have God, through faith, we already have it.

PEACE!
You can reach it too.

12. FLY

They explained to me that an abscess forms when there is an infection, often caused by bacteria, viruses, or even fungi.

It can become inflamed, and you may feel it, or it may appear in other parts of your body.

It becomes a painful pocket filled with pus. The infection can affect an entire area.

Depending on its severity, sometimes it can be treated with a drawing salve. But that doesn't always help. Our body fights it and tries to reject it, but when it can't find a way out naturally, it causes harm. A person may feel their whole body become ill, and they may even develop a fever.

Sometimes, a visit to your family doctor - or even surgery at the hospital - becomes necessary to drain the infection or cut the abscess open to let the pus out.

Once the abscess is eliminated, the person immediately starts to feel better. The infection is out, and the body is clean again so the wound can heal.

I immediately thought about how many times I had these kinds of infections in my body.

Each time, it would appear in another part of me. At different times, they were able to draw the pus out with a drawing salve. Until one day, I had one that had grown on the surface, about the size of an old two-and-a-half-guilder dutch coin with a root that, the doctor told me after surgery, was nearly five centimeters deep. Before I got to my family doctor, who immediately sent me to the hospital, I had a fever, I couldn't walk, and I almost fainted from the pain. Under anesthesia, they were able to remove it completely.

After that surgery, it never came back.

In the same way, our thought patterns can affect our entire lives. Our emotions and actions flow from them. Just as an abscess can affect a physical area, our negative thoughts - about ourselves, others, or situations - can affect parts of our inner world.

If we don't remove them, they can cause harm.

The solution comes when we genuinely deal with our thoughts and emotions.

Our way of thinking must change.

It is important to find a new way to look back at the things we've been through; to reflect, draw wisdom from experience, and begin the work on forgiveness.

We must build a new perspective that strengthens us.

Otherwise, the negative thoughts we refuse to release - and continue to feed - will cause inner complications because we didn't address them in time.

And so, little by little, but surely, we can feel like we're losing our grip and control over our thoughts.

This eventually influences our actions.

We may feel as though we're falling into an "abyss" and cannot see a way out.

This impacts our life and the lives of those we love dearly.

If we truly want to get out of that place of pain, negativity, disappointment, and all those other emotions and feelings, something radical must happen.

Dealing with these things is hard and painful, especially when we've chosen to ignore them for so long. It requires a change in how we think and see our situations.

Confronting the problem becomes essential and even unavoidable.

When you face the reality of your experiences, draw meaningful insights from lived experience and find the good within them, unmasking your scars. Your scars unveiled!

What came to mark you is now what you use for your growth.

Once you overcome it, you can uplift others.

When we remove an abscess, what becomes important is how we care for the wound.

Cleanliness and hygiene are essential while the wound is still open and healing.

This does not mean that just because you are addressing the situation, the pain is gone.

This is a tough process, but when healed, it brings permanent relief.

The scar remains.

It takes time to retrain yourself and take responsibility for your actions without blaming others.

That means "making it part of you" and "owning it."

Accepting it. Deciding that you want it to work for your good.

Not allowing the experiences, situations, or people to negatively change who you are, even when it was unjust, even when others contributed or were at fault.

You can decide how long you will allow the situation or person to dominate your life and control who you become. Holding onto resentment or revenge keeps you in pain and anger, even though you may appear to have moved on.

This requires a paradigm shift, one that leads to different actions.

It means getting out of the victim mindset.

Getting out of the self-pity role.

What came to break you no longer has you broken.

You have dealt with it.

You have recognized it.

You have understood it.

You have learned from the process.

In other words, your scars have unveiled the truth. You have stripped it of its disguise.

And so... just like that... after the long and heavy journey, you have learned a new way to face situations.

What you initially experienced as a burden, now, after you've addressed it and changed your thinking makes you a more complete person.

The wounds heal, and you are left with a mark.

A scar.

You have experience for yourself

and for others.

The scar is the evidence that you went to war.

The situations wounded you, but they also shaped you.

Yet you overcame and gained victory.

The scars now closed remain and become part of who you are.

They fulfilled their purpose.

You have a story.

Nothing was wasted.

What I can tell you from my own experience is that God works all things for good.

Yes, even the things that went wrong or had been snatched from you.

Because you love Him.

He called you according to His purpose.

Your life has purpose.

There is no purpose without suffering.

God loves you, and He never abandons you, not even in your darkest and most difficult moments.

The issues surrounding your life move Him.

You are not alone.

He is there!

Do not confuse what people have done to you or said to you with how God sees you.

He is present.

Every moment.

He wants our happiness, not our downfall.

Nothing can separate you from the love of God.

He heals you because He loves you.

He is there!

Come close to Him, knowing that nothing is impossible for Him.

But we also have a part to play.

It is important that we are honest with ourselves, with others, and certainly with God.

There is hope!

The moment will come when these things no longer have power over you.

You will learn to use your wings to fly...

You will fly... above every situation!

You will tell and use your story to build, empower, and help others.

You have wings on your back. FLY!

www.ingramcontent.com/pod-product-compliance
Lightning Source LLC
Chambersburg PA
CBHW021621120626
46545CB00001B/338